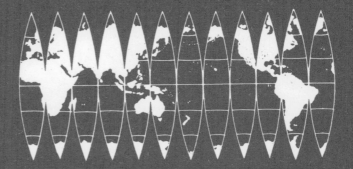

Editor in Chief • PHILLIP BACON

Professor of Geography
Teachers College, Columbia University

Managing Editor • JOANNA ALDENDORFF

Associate Editor • PETER R. LIMBURG

Picture Editor • ROBERT J. GARLOCK

Picture Researcher • PETER J. GALLAGHER

Cartographer • VINCENT KOTSCHAR

Designer • FRANCES GIANNONI

Staff • JUDY KORMAN, BARBARA VINSON, KATHLEEN SEAGRAVES, JOHANNA GREENWALD

Special Section of Statistical Maps • RICHARD EDES HARRISON

Covers • RAY PIOCH

Complete List of Books

These books tell the exciting story of how people live in all parts of the world. You will see how men use the land for farming and industry. You will learn about mountains and deserts, oceans and rivers, cities and towns—and you will discover how the daily life of people in other countries compares with your own.

BOOK 4

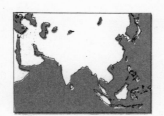

ASIA

BY DOROTHY W. FURMAN
Bureau of Curriculum Research,
New York City Public Schools

THE GOLDEN BOOK

PICTURE ATLAS
OF THE WORLD

IN SIX VOLUMES

Illustrated with More than 1,000 Color Photographs and Maps

GOLDEN PRESS · NEW YORK

Snow-capped Fujiyama, Japan's highest mountain, is a national symbol for Japan's 93,000,000 people.

THIS IS ASIA

Asia is the world's largest continent. Nearly one and a half billion people—more than half the world's population — live there. Asia has more kinds of people, more kinds of land, and more kinds of climate than any other continent. A space traveler flying miles above the earth might be able to see all of Asia at one time. He would see that Europe is connected to Asia but is very much smaller. He would see also that Asia is much larger than Europe and Africa put together, or North and South America together. Asia covers almost one third of the earth's land surface.

Our imaginary space traveler would see many strange and different landscapes. Asia has more mountains than any other continent. Plateaus and mountain ranges criss-cross the central part of Asia. The plateaus are higher than most mountains in other places, and the mountain peaks are thousands of feet higher still. Even the clouds are below the mountain tops. In summer these mountains are covered with ice and snow. The physical maps of Asia on pages 292 to 295 will show you where the mountains are. These maps will help you understand why this part of Asia is called the "roof of the world."

There are thousands of miles of desert too. Some are hot all year round. Others are very cold. Deserts stretch from the Red Sea to Mongolia. Very few people live in the deserts. Water is scarce. The people must wander from place to place in search of grass to feed their flocks.

Great, dark evergreen forests cover northern Asia. Only a small number of hardy people live here. They hunt animals for fur or cut the trees for lumber. Still farther north are the frozen Arctic plains. It is so cold that the land is frozen solid most of the year. Only mosses and lichens can grow. And only a few wandering tribes live here with their herds of reindeer.

South of the frozen tundra and the evergreen forests are thousands of miles of grassland. Cattle graze and millions of bushels of wheat are grown.

Farther to the south are the hot, rainy lands. Here in the steaming jungles live tigers, elephants, monkeys, and tropical birds. Millions of people live in the hot lands. Some live in tiny crowded villages and farm the rich soil along the river banks. Over the world, the greatest numbers of people live close to water.

In east Asia too, millions of people live on little farms close to the rivers. Some live on river boats and even grow food there. Others live in cities more crowded than any other place in the world. But the high, dry central part of Asia is bare. Very few people can live there.

To the east, on the islands of Japan, farms are planted even on the sides of mountains. Japan is so crowded that every available inch of land is used for food. Still not enough food is grown.

On many islands south of Asia it rains most of the year. These islands are covered with hot tropical jungles. Some islands grow rubber, coffee, sugar, tea, and spices.

With the highest mountains and the lowest depressions in the world, tropical heat and arctic cold, dense rainforests and barren deserts—Asia is truly a continent of great contrasts.

Utilizing every bit of land, Philippine farmers grow rice on carefully terraced hillsides.

A. Kolb, Hamburg

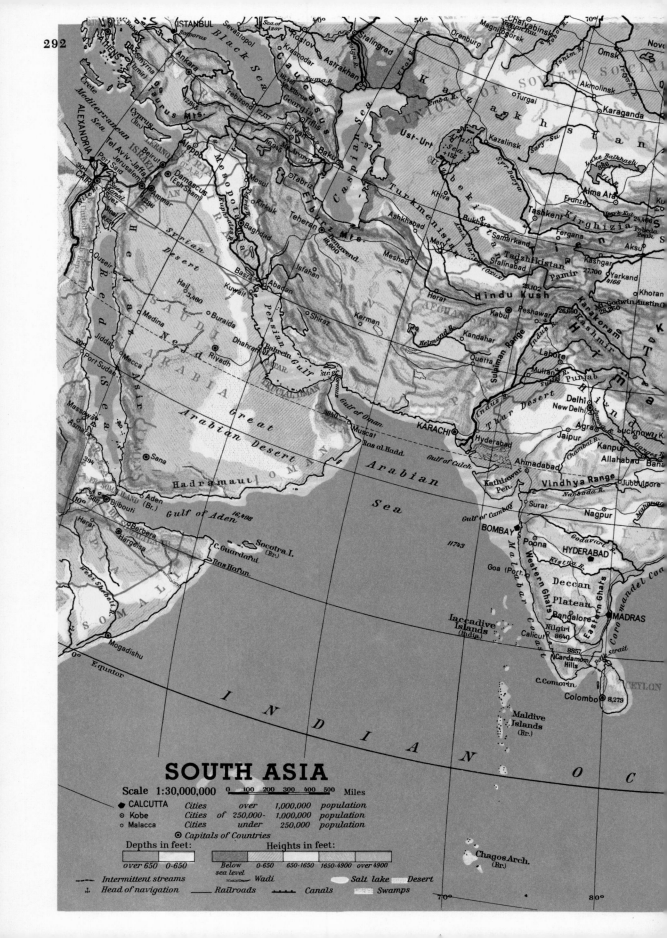

SOUTH ASIA

Scale 1:30,000,000 |0 100 200 300 400 500   Miles

◆ **CALCUTTA**   *Cities*   *over*   *1,000,000*   *population*
⊙ Kobe   *Cities*   *of* 250,000-   *1,000,000*   *population*
○ Malacca   *Cities*   *under*   *250,000*   *population*
⊙ *Capitals of Countries*

Depths in feet: Heights in feet:

over 650   0-650   Below sea level   0-650   650-1650   1650-4900   over 4900

---- *Intermittent streams*   ___ *Wadi*   *Salt lake*   *Desert*
⊥ *Head of navigation*   ___ *Railroads*   ···· *Canals*   *Swamps*

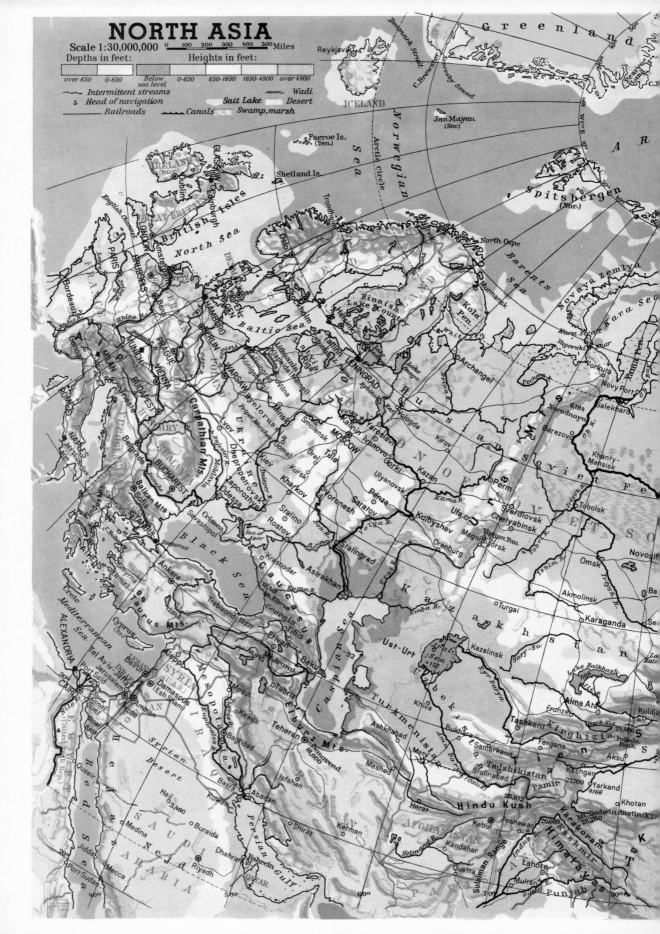

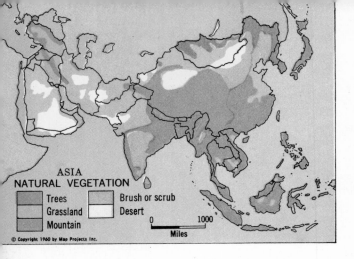

Your map shows you that the continents of Asia and Europe are connected. Together they make up a large land mass called Eurasia. But Asia alone measures about seventeen million square miles. This is approximately one third of the earth's land surface. From north to south Asia stretches from 85 degrees north latitude (well inside the Arctic Circle) to 10 degrees south latitude (south of the equa-

tor). From Turkey in the west, Asia extends eastward to the Bering Straits, a range of longitude from 25 degrees east to 170 degrees west. This distance measures almost halfway around the earth.

Many seas and oceans touch Asia's vast continent. To the north lies the cold Arctic Ocean. The Mediterranean, the Black and the Red seas wash Asia's western shores. To the south are the warm Indian Ocean, the Arabian Sea and the Bay of Bengal. Eastern Asia fronts on the Pacific Ocean. Many smaller seas, really branches of the Pacific, touch Asia on the east. There are the Bering Sea, the Sea of Japan, the Yellow Sea, the Sea of Okhotsk, and the South China Sea. Your map of Asia will show you many other bordering bodies of water.

Ships from Europe, the United States, and other parts of the world still use the seas and oceans to reach Asia's coastal regions. The opening of the Suez Canal in

The glacier-gouged Karakoram Mountains in central Asia contain some of the world's highest peaks.

K. Paffen

H. Spreitzer

Wheat is raised on the treeless, hilly steppes of the Anatolian Plateau in Turkey.

1869 made it easier for European ships to trade with much of coastal Asia. Today air transportation, especially connections between Asia and North America across the north polar regions, is opening up many parts of central Asia to trade and travel.

Unlike other continents, the heart of Asia is a mass of great mountain ranges and high, bleak plateaus. There are no fertile lowlands in the central part of Asia similar to the Mississippi River valley in North America. Central Asia is high, mountainous, cold, bleak, and very, very hard to reach.

If all the chief mountain ranges and plateaus in central Asia were grouped together, they would stretch for about 5,000 miles. They make up the largest group of mountains and highlands in the world. These mountains, together with the deserts that lie between many of the ranges, make central Asia a very inhospitable place for outsiders to reach.

Some of the world's greatest river systems have their sources in the mountains of central Asia. Melting snows from the

slopes of mountain ranges—the Hindu Kush, Pamirs, Elburz, Karakoram, Altyn Tagh, Tien Shan, and Himalaya—pour downward to form rivers and streams. The Ob, Yenisei and Lena Rivers rise in the mountains of northern Asia. They flow

Encroaching sand dunes threaten to cover this date-palm oasis in the deserts of Saudi Arabia.

Aramco—Photo Researchers

Courtesy of TWA—Trans World Airlines

Ceylon's warm, wet climate and rich soils favor rice-growing. These women plant rice by hand.

Southern China has rugged terrain. Farms are crowded into the valleys between the craggy hills.

Van Bucher—Photo Researchers

northward and empty into the Arctic Ocean. Few people are able to live in the cold, northern lowlands of these rivers. Other rivers, such as the Indus, Ganges, Irrawaddy, Mekong, Brahmaputra, Salween, Yangtze, and Hwang Ho, begin in the mountains and flow to the east, south and west. Millions of Asians make their homes in the hot, fertile valleys through which these rivers flow to reach the Pacific and Indian Oceans. In western Asia, the Tigris and Euphrates join to empty into the Persian Gulf. Today, as in ancient times, this river system provides water for irrigation.

Some rivers in Asia never reach the sea. Instead, they flow through hundreds of miles of steppe and desert land. Finally they empty into great salt swamps, or into inland seas and lakes such as Lake Balkhash, Lake Aral and the Caspian Sea.

Below: monsoon rains feed the waterways along which nine tenths of Thailand's people live.

Above: tropical vegetation grows luxuriantly in the lowlands of Bengal, in India's northeast.

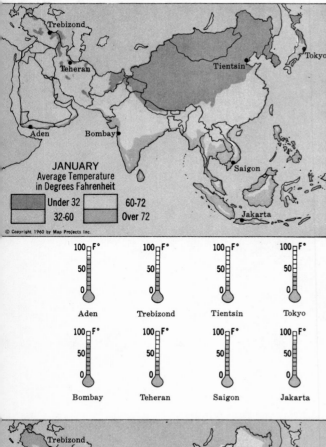

JANUARY
Average Temperature
in Degrees Fahrenheit

| Under 32 | 60-72 |
| 32-60 | Over 72 |

© Copyright 1960 by Map Projects Inc.

Aden   Trebizond   Tientsin   Tokyo

Bombay   Teheran   Saigon   Jakarta

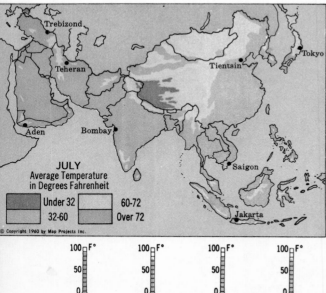

JULY
Average Temperature
in Degrees Fahrenheit

| Under 32 | 60-72 |
| 32-60 | Over 72 |

© Copyright 1960 by Map Projects Inc.

Aden   Trebizond   Tientsin   Tokyo

Bombay   Teheran   Saigon   Jakarta

CLIMATE

Asia stretches about 5,000 miles from north of the Arctic Circle to south of the equator. From east to west Asia stretches nearly halfway around the world. This vast area has many different kinds of climate. Asia has some of the coldest and some of the hottest, some of the wettest and some of the driest places in the world.

The great interior lands of Asia are far from the ocean. Winds from the oceans are cut off by the high mountain chains which surround the interior. Because of this, the climate of central Asia is one of extremes. Winters are long and cold, chilled by cold winds from the polar regions. Summers everywhere but the highlands are short and hot. Except in the mountains, there is little rainfall. Consequently, much of the region is desert.

Northern Asia has much the same sort of climate as central Asia, except that it has more rainfall. Winters are extremely cold—the coldest inhabited place in the world is a village in Siberia called Verkhoyansk. The temperature there sometimes drops to 90 degrees below zero.

In southern Asia the climate is quite different. Here it is hot all year round, except in the mountains. The temperature in the lowlands may reach as high as 125 degrees. There are no summer and winter as we know them. Instead, there is a rainy season and a dry season.

The rainy season usually lasts from June through October. During that period it rains heavily every day. More rain falls in this part of Asia than in any other place in the world. Some areas in India get more than 450 inches of rainfall during the rainy season.

The rainy and dry seasons are caused by winds called monsoons, which blow over most of Asia. In winter the monsoons blow from central Asia toward the southern and eastern edges of the continent. Winter monsoons are dry winds because they blow over dry land. They are cold because they come from a cold region. The summer monsoons blow inland from the oceans, bringing moisture as far inland as they reach.

The rainy season is very important to the millions of people who live in southern and eastern Asia. This is the season when they plant the crops on which they depend for their food. Without the rains the plants will not grow. Drought brings famine, and thousands of people starve. Sometimes the monsoons are late, and crops cannot be planted in time to ripen. Sometimes the monsoons bring floods.

Southwestern Asia is another very dry region. Summers there are long and very hot. Winters are relatively mild except in the far interior. In certain areas of southwestern Asia, winter is the rainy season. It is also the growing season, because crops would die in the hot, dry summers.

Climate has a great influence on the way people live. For example, the people of northern Siberia live in a region of long, extremely cold winters and short summers. The soil is permanently frozen beneath the surface, making farming impossible. The natives of northern Siberia must depend for their living on hunting and fishing.

In Burma the climate is warm and there is abundant rainfall. In the rainy season there are floods; so the people living near rivers build their houses on stilts to escape the flood waters. The warm, wet climate is ideal for raising rice; so most of the people are farmers, and rice is the chief food.

Afghanistan is a dry, mountainous inland country. The roughness of the terrain leaves little land fit for cultivation, and the rainfall is not enough to support crops. Because of this, farming is limited to the river valleys and oases (fed by melting snows from the mountains), where there is enough water for irrigation and enough level land for cultivation. Many people raise sheep for their meat and wool, because sheep are hardy animals which can get along on scanty forage and little water.

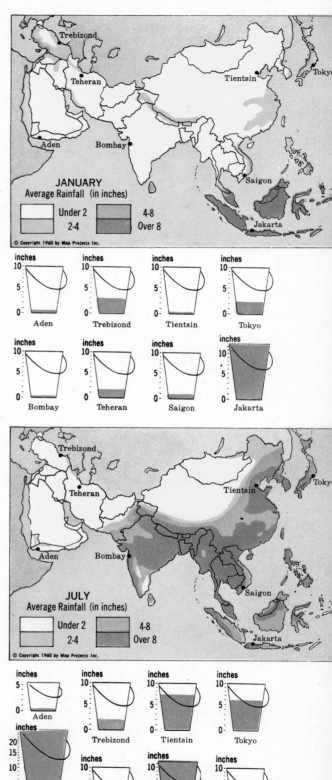

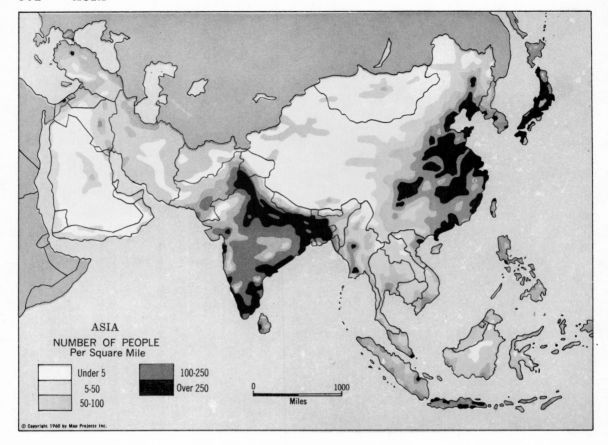

ASIA
NUMBER OF PEOPLE
Per Square Mile

Under 5	100-250
5-50	Over 250
50-100	

0   1000
Miles

© Copyright 1960 by Map Projects Inc.

ASIA'S PEOPLE

A continent as vast as Asia is bound to have great variations between its regions. There are differences in climate, landforms, and animal and plant life. But perhaps the greatest difference of all is between the many groups of people who live in Asia. Almost every racial type in the world can be found there.

There is every variety of skin color, from white through yellow and brown to black, and every shade between. There is an equally great variety of physical types and facial appearances. These different types of body builds and features are found in every "race" or skin-color group. For thousands of years various groups have been mixing, creating ever new combinations of characteristics.

Much more significant than the physical differences between Asia's peoples are the cultural differences — the way they live,

Julien Bryan—Photo Researchers

Turbaned Afghan men watch a **coronation parade** in Kabul, the capital of Afghanistan.

These men are Jordanian Arabs. Arabs are the largest group of people in southwestern Asia.

their habits and customs, the religions they believe in, their values, the languages they speak, the way they think. These differences, like physical differences, also cut across racial lines.

In southwest Asia, for example, most of the people are Caucasian, or "white." Yet there are great differences in the way they look and the way they live. Arabs, Turks, Persians, Kurds, and Israelis all speak different languages, dress differently, and

have different ideas of what is good and what is bad. They follow different religions. The Turks, the Persians, and most of the Arabs are Moslems. Some of the Arabs are Christians. And most Israelis are Jewish. Each religion has many sects. Even within such a group as the Arabs, who speak the same language, there are great differences between the desert nomads with their flocks, the settled farmers of the more fertile regions, and the townsmen.

With great toil the people of Israel have turned barren desert into flourishing farmland.

An Arab rug merchant squats by his wares in the marketplace of Kuwait on the Persian Gulf.

In south Asia there are even more differences between groups of people. In India alone fourteen major languages are spoken (the total number of languages and dialects is 845). In religion, most Indians are Hindus, but there are also Moslems, Sikhs, Jains, Christians, Buddhists, and Zoroastrians (fire-worshippers).

The same sorts of differences can be found in the other parts of Asia. What makes the people so different from each other? Part of the answer is tradition—the customs and beliefs handed down from generation to generation. Another reason is the values taught by their religions.

Still another reason for the differences is the influence of the surroundings—climate, landforms, nature of the soil, and natural resources. It is clear that people who live in a cold, dry region of grasslands and deserts, like the Mongols, will live very differently from the people of a wet tropical island such as Java.

The wide, rolling grasslands of Mongolia are ideal for herding livestock. The Mongols have traditionally spent their lives following their herds, living on meat and milk.

The people of Java can raise good crops on the fertile soil of their island. They have solved the problem of mountainous terrain by building terraces on the slopes. On these artificial flatlands they raise their food.

But Java is very crowded, and there is not enough land to raise food for both the people and large numbers of animals. So the Javanese live mostly on rice. They get most of their protein from fish.

Israel, where Jews from all over the world have settled, was formerly a land of deserts and swamps. Great efforts were

Hindu pilgrims bathe in the Ganges River at Benares in order to acquire spiritual merit.

Valentina Rosen

Michel Serraillier—Rapho Guillumette
A Kashmir merchant serves his customers.

Lowber Tiers—Monkmeyer
Smiling Malayan children lead a carefree life.

necessary to drain the swamps and irrigate the deserts so that people could live there and develop farms and industries.

Because Asia is large and communications (until recently) have been very poor, the people of each district developed their own dialect or local variety of a language. Often the dialects of the same language may be so different that two people speaking different dialects cannot understand each other. Thus, a Chinese from Canton may not be able to understand another Chinese from a village only 50 miles away.

The fact that so many Asian people speak different dialects or languages has

This saffron-robed Thai youth is a Buddhist monk.
Herbert Knapp

Ed Lettau—Shostal
A Pakistani snake-charmer puts on his act.

Straw coolie hat shields Vietnamese girl from sun.
Fujihira—Monkmeyer

children. In the Philippines, where the people speak various Malayan dialects, the official dialect is Tagalog.

Religion deeply affects the daily lives of people in Asia, both through its commandments and its influence on their outlook on life. For instance, Hindus, because they hold the cow sacred, are forbidden to eat beef or injure cattle in any way. Very religious Hindus will not eat any kind of meat and will not kill any living creature, even if it is a harmful one.

In the past, Hindus have been forbidden to marry out of their own religious caste.

George Holton—Photo Library

Tibetan porters carry 300-pound loads of tea and other goods up mountain paths from China.

caused a great deal of difficulty for the governments of Asian countries. To overcome this problem, some countries have established one dialect or language as the official one. In India, for example, the official language is Hindi. In China the Mandarin dialect is taught to all school

John Strohm

This Mongol woman's ancestors once ruled a mighty empire that covered most of Asia.

An old lady of Peking tends her young grandchild. In China, 55,000 babies are born every day.

John Strohm

This Communist soldier symbolizes China's determination to become a great power.

John Strohm

Ewing Krainin—Photo Researchers

This Javanese man's red fez shows that he is a Moslem, as are nine out of ten Indonesians.

Ernst A. Heiniger

A Japanese father gives his child a lesson in the tricky technique of handling chopsticks.

Even the type of work they were allowed to do, the food they ate, and the clothes they wore were determined by the caste to which they belonged. However, this is now changing as India becomes more modern and industrialized.

Until the Communists came to power in China, most Chinese worshipped the spirits of their ancestors. This led them to feel great reverence for the past and for traditional ways of doing things. This respect for the methods used by their fathers and grandfathers has often made the Chinese unwilling to adopt newer and better methods.

Mankind has lived in Asia a very long time. Some of the oldest known fossils of prehistoric man have been found on the island of Java in Indonesia and near Peking in northern China. The world's oldest civilizations are Asian. Chinese civilization is nearly 5,000 years old, and the civilization of India is nearly that old.

Anthropologists, or students of mankind, say that the oldest civilization of all, and the ancestor of our civilization, was located in the region called Mesopotamia, between the Tigris and Euphrates rivers in southwest Asia.

Asia has had great influence on the western nations. The very important inventions of papermaking, printing, and gunpowder, for example, all came from China. The learning of the Greeks and Romans was preserved for hundreds of years during the Dark Ages by Arab scholars in southwest Asia. And it was the search for a sea route to the spice markets of India that led Columbus to discover America.

The Philippine government is trying to put education within reach of all children.

Harrison Forman—Shostal

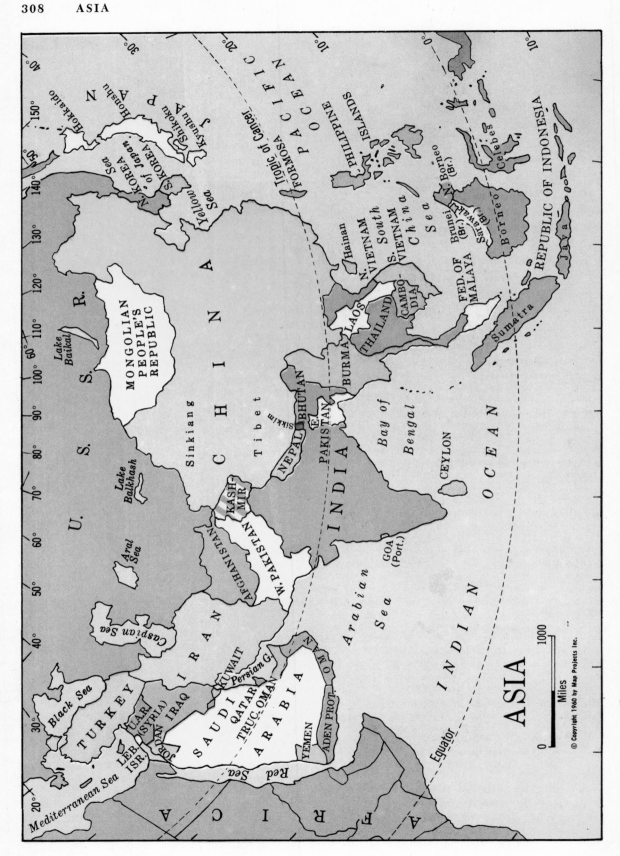

ASIA

Miles

0   1000

© Copyright 1960 by Map Projects Inc.

TRANSPORTATION

There are more than 30 countries in Asia today. Many have changed their names or forms of government since World War II. Some, like Israel, did not even exist a few years ago. Others which once belonged to European nations are independent. Some are monarchies, like Japan. Others, like the Philippines, are republics. Some, though self-governing, are also members of the British Commonwealth. Some, like the Chinese People's Republic (China) and North Korea, are Communist-controlled.

People in the United States and Europe are able to travel quickly from one place to another, even when the places are hundreds of miles apart. There are many good roads, railroads, and airlines to choose from.

In Asia travel is very different. Asia has extremes of surface and climate, so that overland travel is often difficult. High mountains, plateaus, deserts, and jungles make it almost impossible to build roads and railroads in many places.

Few railroads go directly from one country to another. Many people in Asia have never seen or traveled on a railroad. In fact most of them have never traveled more than a few miles from the tiny villages where they were born.

Some countries do have good railroads. India's railway lines were built by the British. Japan, too, has many fine railroads.

Highways are even fewer than railroads in Asia. Southwest Asia has no paved roads leading to southern Asia. There are some trails leading north from India through the mountains to Tibet or China, but cars, trucks, and even wagons are unable to travel on them. The Burma Road is passable for only a few months of the year.

Fortunately, in recent years there has been rapid growth in air transportation in Asia. Several major airlines now connect countries of Southern Asia with Europe and the United States. Airlines make regular stops at Manila, Hong Kong, Tokyo, Bom-

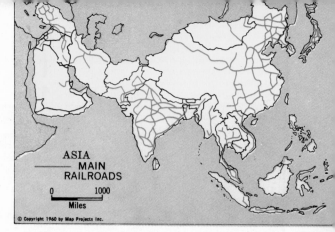

ASIA MAIN RAILROADS

0   1000
Miles
© Copyright 1960 by Map Projects Inc.

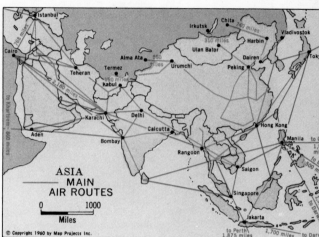

ASIA MAIN AIR ROUTES

0   1000
Miles
© Copyright 1960 by Map Projects Inc.

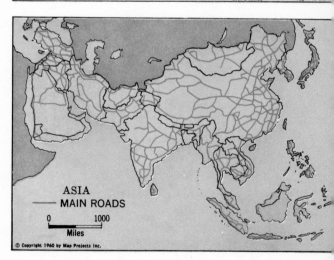

ASIA MAIN ROADS

0   1000
Miles
© Copyright 1960 by Map Projects Inc.

bay, Calcutta, Rangoon, and Ankara. But the vast central part of Asia has no air service, just as it has few roads or railroads.

Look at the rail map, the highway map, and the air route map on page 309. Compare them with the political map of Asia on page 308. From them you can tell which countries have the best transportation.

Istanbul, the largest city of Turkey, is located in Turkey's European portion.

CITIES OF ASIA

Just as Asia has many kinds of climate, surfaces, and people, so it has different kinds of cities. Some cities are more than 1,000 years old, with sections that look the way they did long ago. Others have modern buildings and houses. Many European and American business firms have offices in these Asian cities. Pictures on pages 310 to 313 show you some typical scenes in the great cities of Asia. Here are some facts about Asia's major cities.

Tokyo is the capital of Japan. It is the world's largest city. Tokyo is the center of Japan's industry and culture.

Tokyo does a great deal of business with the United States and the rest of the world. It has a deep-water harbor nearby. Several major airlines stop at Tokyo. Textiles, ships, and automobiles, as well as toys, cameras, and optical goods are a few of Tokyo's exports. Thousands of tourists visit Tokyo each year, especially during the cherry blossom season.

Peking is the capital of the Chinese People's Republic (Communist China). This is one of China's oldest cities.

Peking's main industries are steel, machinery, and textiles. All the industries are controlled by the government.

Shanghai is China's largest city and seaport. Shanghai is on the Whangpoo River, inland from the coast. It supplies goods to the millions of Chinese who live in villages and farms throughout the crowded Yangtze River valley.

Shanghai has the largest textile industry in China. It also produces ships, machinery, and food products.

Tientsin is another important Chinese port city. It is 70 miles southeast of Peking.

Tientsin is the commercial center for north China, second only to Shanghai in the manufacture of cloth. Several important railroad lines meet in Tientsin. Thus it is the gateway to the inland region and to Peking, the capital of Communist China.

HONG KONG is a British crown colony. It consists of a little island off the coast of China and a small portion of the mainland, called Kowloon. It has a fine deepwater harbor where ships from all over the world come to trade. Most of the docks and businesses that line the shore of the island are owned by British companies.

The mainland, which is only a mile away, is connected with Hong Kong Island by ferries, and thousands of workers commute from the mainland. Hong Kong is supported mostly by foreign trade. There are many related businesses such as insurance, banking, warehousing, and ship repairing.

BOMBAY is on India's west coast. It is India's second largest city, on an island a short distance from the mainland, with which it is connected by bridges. Bombay's harbor is one of the world's finest.

Bombay became an important cotton center during the Civil War in America,

Wendy Hilty—Monkmeyer

Minarets tower over the main square of Baghdad, capital of Iraq and once seat of an empire.

Bombay, India's second-largest city, is a bustling, modern metropolis.

Courtesy of TWA—Trans World Airlines

Hamilton Wright Organization Inc.

Above: Hong Kong has modern office buildings and residences, but the poor live in slums.

Ray Halin—Shostal

Above: Saigon, the capital of South Vietnam, shows both European and Oriental styles.

Paul Hufner—Shostal

when England could not get cotton from the Southern states. Today it is India's leading cotton-manufacturing city. Later, the Suez Canal made it still easier for European ships to trade with Bombay.

CALCUTTA is India's largest city. It is on the Ganges delta, about 80 miles inland from the Bay of Bengal. Calcutta, a leading manufacturing center, is its most important eastern city.

One of Calcutta's chief products and exports is burlap. Burlap is made from jute, grown nearby. Many products, including coffee, tea, rubber, cotton, and hemp, are exported through Calcutta. Railways link Calcutta to other cities in India.

JAKARTA is the capital of the Republic of Indonesia and its largest city. It is a seaport on the north coast of Java. The name itself means "important city." When the Dutch ruled the Indonesian islands, the city was called Batavia.

Jakarta ships the products of the Indonesian islands to countries all over the world. These products include kapok, spices, rubber, sugar, cocoa, coffee, tea, and copra. Most of the industries were once in the hands of the Dutch, but now they are controlled by the Indonesian government.

SAIGON, capital and largest city of South Vietnam, is part of the twin cities of Saigon-Cholon. South Vietnam was once part of French Indo-China.

Because South Vietnam is not under Communist control, the United States and other western countries carry on a good deal of trade with Saigon.

MANILA is the largest and most important city in the Philippine Islands. In addition to Filipinos, there are large numbers of Chinese who have settled there and become citizens. Some people are descended from the Spaniards who ruled the islands before the Spanish-American War. Many Americans have business interests here.

Small barges transport much of the merchandise handled in Shanghai's busy harbor.

In a single year more than 3,000 ships call at Manila. Its leading manufactured exports are rope, cotton textiles, tobacco, and coconut oil.

SEOUL is the capital of South Korea. It is located on the Han River, 19 miles inland from the Yellow Sea. About one and a half million people live there.

Seoul has important manufacturing industries—silk, paper, and tobacco are produced here. During the Korean War many businesses and homes were destroyed.

MUKDEN is the largest city in Manchuria. It is an important manufacturing city in Communist China. Coal and iron in nearby regions supply the factories. One of Mukden's chief products is automobiles.

BAGHDAD, the capital city of Iraq, is located on the Tigris River, 350 miles north of the Persian Gulf. It was once the chief city on the caravan route between Europe and the Far East.

The discovery of oil nearby has made Baghdad a beehive of industry today.

John Strohm

The "Palace of Rest and Culture" in Peking is emblematic of China's Communist rulers.

Ewing Krainin—Alpha

Bright lights and neon signs make downtown Tokyo by night as gay as Broadway.

Jakarta, capital of Indonesia, has varied traffic— bicycles, motorscooters, and pedicabs.

Van Bucher—Photo Researchers

Manila's location on a protected bay has helped it become one of the Orient's great ports.

Ray Halin—Shostal

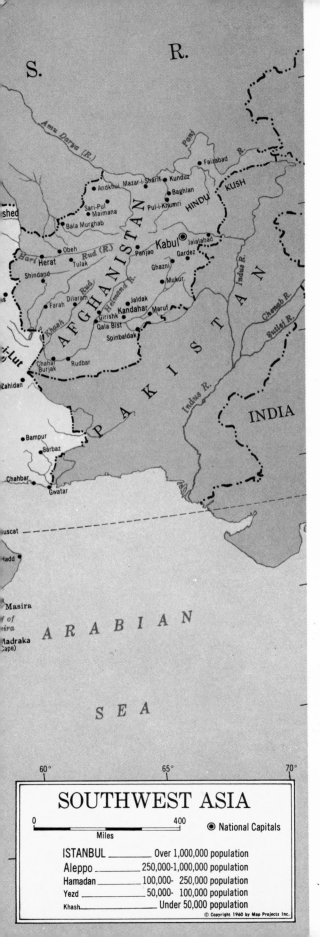

SOUTHWEST ASIA

Southwest Asia is often called the Middle East or Near East. The chief countries in this region are Saudi Arabia, Turkey, Syria, Jordan, Lebanon, Israel, Iraq, and Iran. Afghanistan is sometimes included in this region. In addition there are several small countries on the Arabian peninsula.

Southwest Asia is the place where Asia, Europe, and Africa meet. Since earliest times this has been a crossroad for trade, people, armies, and ideas. Gold, silver, silks, rugs, precious gems, dates, perfumes, spices—all reached Europe by way of southwest Asia. Camel caravans carried goods across central Asia from China, or through mountain passes from India and Afghanistan. Some goods came by boat through the Red Sea.

In ancient times Mongol tribes from Asia invaded Europe by passing through this region. When Greece and Rome were in their glory, armies came from Europe to invade southwest Asia. Later, during the Crusades, Europeans were in the Holy Land and returned home with the products of Asia as well as with new ideas. Three great religions had their start here: Judaism, Christianity, and Islam.

Some scientists believe that this part of the world may have been the original home of man. We do know that civilized man has lived in southwest Asia for a longer time than in any other place in the world.

Weather and climate have had an important effect on southwest Asia. There is very little rain in most parts, and what little rain there is comes in the winter months.

Only on the narrow coastal plains bordering the Mediterranean, Black, and Caspian seas is there much rainfall. The summers are long, hot, and dry. The temperature sometimes reaches 130 degrees. Hot, sand-bearing winds often blow for days at a time.

Most of the interior is desert or dry grassland. In some scattered spots, called oases,

SOUTHWEST ASIA

0 _____ 400
Miles

⊙ National Capitals

ISTANBUL _____ Over 1,000,000 population
Aleppo _____ 250,000-1,000,000 population
Hamadan _____ 100,000- 250,000 population
Yezd _____ 50,000- 100,000 population
Khash_____ Under 50,000 population

© Copyright 1960 by Map Projects Inc.

people can grow crops. Here underground springs irrigate the land, making it possible to grow date palms and grains. Once in a while a little rain falls in the desert and a few scattered bushes and grasses can grow.

Even the river beds are dry during the summer months. Sometimes in the winter months there are short but heavy cloudbursts. Then the dry river beds (called *wadies*) overflow and flood the land.

The floods can wash away houses or even entire villages. But in most of southwest Asia there is less than 10 inches of rainfall a year. The maps on pages 300 and 301 will show you how little rain falls in this region, and how warm it is most of the year. In a few places, particularly Israel, dams and irrigation systems have been built. Here the desert has been turned into fertile farmland.

Southwest Asia is one of the most sparsely settled regions in the world. Nowhere are there densely crowded lands like those in southeast Asia. Only in the cities and in the fertile valley between the Tigris and Euphrates rivers are there many people.

In most of the drier portions of southwest Asia the people are sheep and goat herders. They are nomads, which means they do not live in one place for long. Instead they wander from place to place with their flocks in search of grass.

Many kinds of people live in southwest Asia. There are some Europeans as well as Asians. Most of the people belong to the Caucasian (white) race, though often their skins are quite dark. In general the people in Iraq, Arabia, Lebanon, Jordan, and Syria are Arabs, whose language is Arabic. Their religion is Islam, though large numbers of Lebanese are Christian.

In recent years many of these countries have banded together for political reasons and have joined the Arab League.

Iranians and Turks are also Moslems, but they are not Arabs. Iranians speak Persian, as do some of the people of Afghanistan. The language of the Turks is Turkish.

Hebrew is the official language of Israel, most of whose people are Jews. However, many languages, including Arabic and English, are spoken in Israel. French and English are spoken in many of the cities throughout this part of the world.

Southwest Asia has many serious problems. Most of the people are very poor.

Shepherds still water their flocks at the wells of Jericho, as they did in Biblical times.

A Syrian village clings to the side of an eroded mountain. Its location affords protection from raiders.

Though the rulers have always lived in luxury, they have done little for the welfare of others. Villages are built of sun-dried brick. Houses are crowded and primitive.

Water is scarce and often impure. Sometimes the animals live in the houses with the people. There is little attempt at sanitation. Filth and disease are common. Every kind of tropical illness is found here, but there are few doctors, hospitals, or medicines except in the large cities. There is almost no education. Most of the land is too dry to grow food.

The governments of these countries have done little to correct these conditions. Political problems exist all the time.

Most of the Arab nations resent Israel, and will not co-operate with her. There are frequent border fights between Arabs and Israelis, as well as tribal battles.

Kay Lawson—Rapho Guillumette

Primitive methods of harvesting characterize agriculture in southwestern Asia.

The Fertile Crescent and the Dry Lands

The kind of land on which people live in southwest Asia affects the way they live there. Most of the land is arid (dry) or semi-arid. Only where there is enough water through irrigation can much of the land be farmed. Yet most of the people who live here make their living from the land.

One of the few regions with water for farming is the "Fertile Crescent." It stretches from the Persian Gulf northwest through the Tigris–Euphrates River valley in Iraq. Then it turns west into Syria and then circles southwest into Israel.

The Tigris and Euphrates rivers provide water for irrigation in Iraq. Most of the farmers still use methods hundreds of years

old. River water is spilled into the ditches by old-fashioned water wheels, which are turned by the river current or by animals. Plowing is still done by hand.

Most of the farmers in this region are either sharecroppers or tenant farmers. They lease small plots of land from rich landowners. They pay for the land with a share of their crops. Sometimes the farmer must give a share to the man who supplies the seed, and another share to the man who furnishes the water for irrigation.

The tenant farmer cannot afford to fertilize or improve land which he does not own. Often the landowner is a money lender as well. The poor farmer finds himself heavily in debt.

Barley, wheat, rice, and other grains, as well as cotton and tobacco, are grown in the river valley. Dates are an important crop, too. The Shatt-al-Arab region in southern Iraq, near the Persian Gulf, raises four fifths of the world's dates.

In this region a natural type of irrigation is used. Tides in the Persian Gulf rise twice each day. These rising tides push the fresh water of the river back into irrigation ditches. When the tides fall the water drains back into the river. This natural irrigation is controlled by gates which are opened and shut to regulate the water.

The Euphrates River supplies water for irrigated farms like this Syrian cottonfield.

Samy Abboud—FPG

Mechanized farming is little known in Asia. Animals are the chief source of power.

Rupert Leach—FPG

A Turkish woman gathers rose petals, the essence of which will be extracted for perfume.

Dates are an important food in southwest Asia, as well as an export product.

However, there are several large land areas in the river valley which cannot be used for farming. Poor drainage makes some places marshy and swampy. Other sections are in constant danger of flooding. Flood control, water storage, and drainage projects are now being developed.

Here and there throughout southwest Asia's desert lands there are fertile oases, places with water. Sometimes the water comes from underground springs. Sometimes it comes from a nearby river. Oases may be just a few acres in size, or they may be several miles across. Villages often grow up near oases. Nomads stop to rest and to water their flocks. Traders bring goods to sell or trade. Date palms provide food as well as shade. In larger oases, crops are planted.

The Damascus oasis in Syria is one of the largest and oldest irrigated places in the world. Wheat, barley, corn, rice, olives, vegetables, and fruit are grown. Unlike most land in southwest Asia, the land is owned by the farmers, not big landowners.

In Iran farming methods are also old-fashioned. Most farm work is done by hand, and very little machinery is used. Much of the land is too mountainous for farming. In the lowlands water is brought for irrigation by a system of underground channels which carry water from sources miles away in the mountains.

Wheat, barley, and rice are the main crops, though a good deal of cotton is also grown. Fruits, vegetables, and dairy products are important foods raised. In the mountains semi-nomadic people pasture their flocks during the summer months.

Child labor is common in the Near East. This Iranian girl strings tobacco for drying.

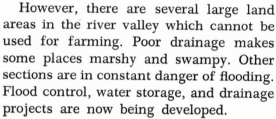

Israeli schoolchildren learn about farming in the fields of their farm settlement.

Israel has introduced modern farming methods and machinery. More and more land is being reclaimed from the deserts and swamps. Farm settlements, called *kibbutzim*, train thousands of new settlers each year. Dams and reservoirs which Israel hopes to build on the Jordan River will irrigate many more sections.

The Negev, the desert region of southern Israel, contains millions of acres of land which can be irrigated. Water is being brought to some parts by pipelines from reservoirs miles away.

Israel raises a variety of fruits and vegetables, livestock, poultry, and dairy products. Oranges and grapes are important crops, too. Israel is planting thousands of trees on the barren hills. Within a few years, forests will help prevent the soil from eroding, or washing away.

Oranges and lemons, exported fresh and in juice concentrates, are major products of Israel.

Israel's farmers use modern machinery. Below: a wheat crop in Israel is being harvested.

Roubat—Monkmeyer

Kurdish nomads wander the mountains of the Iran-Iraq border, seeking grass and water.

Much of the land outside the Fertile Crescent is too dry for farming. In some parts of southwest Asia nothing at all will grow. In semi-arid sections there are scattered pasture lands with enough grass to feed flocks of sheep, goats, and camels.

The Bedouins of the Arabian peninsula raise sheep, goats, camels, and horses. The Bedouins depend almost entirely on their flocks for their living. The milk of sheep, goats, and camels is their chief food. When there is no more grass in one place, the tribe packs up and moves on.

Sometimes a tribe stops at an oasis for several weeks. They trade animals, hides, and wool for food, cloth, and weapons. Soon they move on to find new pasture land. Nomadic tribes sometimes fight each other for control of grazing land or springs.

In some parts of southwest Asia rain falls in the winter months. This is true in the lands bordering the Mediterranean, especially parts of Turkey, Syria, and Lebanon. These lands are said to have a "mediterranean" climate. Because the winters are mild, wheat and barley can be planted in the fall and harvested in spring.

During the hot, dry summer months, dry-farming methods are used in some places. The soil is plowed deep and fine. Then it is packed firmly around the roots of plants. Water deep underground is soaked up. The surface of the soil is covered with a thick layer of loose, dry soil. This layer keeps the water underneath from evaporating and makes it possible to grow summer crops.

For the most part though, farming must depend on irrigation. Where water can be found, cotton, olives, barley, mulberry trees (for feeding silkworms), potatoes, tobacco, vegetables, and fruits can be raised.

Boubat, Realites—Photo Researchers

This Jordanian shepherd keeps a protective eye on his herd as it crosses barren land.

Courtesy of TWA—Trans World Airlines

A pipeline to a prospective oil well stretches through the desert. Oil is piped from the fields to the Mediterranean for shipment to other countries.

The ungainly camel is familiar in all desert areas —even those occupied by oil wells.

John Strohm

Oil—Wealth from the Desert

Southwest Asia has the world's largest known supply of petroleum. Oil fields stretch from the Persian Gulf into the valley of the Tigris-Euphrates.

The greatest oil deposits are in Iraq, Iran, Saudi Arabia, Kuwait, Bahrein, and Qatar. This part of Asia produces more than one billion barrels of oil each year. This is nearly one fourth of all the oil produced in the world. New discoveries are made each year. No one knows how much oil lies beneath the deserts of southwest Asia.

Most of the oil fields are run by British or American oil companies, which rent land from the governments. They drill wells and build pipelines which carry the oil across the deserts to seaports on the Mediterranean or on the Persian Gulf. There the oil is piped into tankers and shipped to refineries in the United States and Great Britain.

Southwest Asia's oil has great political importance. Western European countries get most of the oil they need from southwest Asia. Large amounts of European and American money are invested in the oil fields. Thus it is important for these countries to stay friendly with the oil-producing nations of southwest Asia.

Because of the importance of oil, the Soviet Union has been trying to get control of some of these rich oil fields. Southwest Asia has, therefore, become more and more important in world affairs.

The discovery and production of oil depends on highly trained American and British engineers. But much of the day-to-day work is now being carried on by Arabs. They have been trained to drive trucks, to serve as mechanics, and to operate wells, pipelines, and pumping stations.

The oil fields look very different from other parts of southwest Asia. Derricks, refineries, pipelines, pumping stations, and huge tanks appear in the desert. Towns have been built for native workers as well as for Americans and Europeans.

Iranian Oil Participants Ltd.

Aramco—Photo Researchers

Above left: an up-to-date oilcracking installation at Abadan, Iran, helps refine the oil of the Persian Gulf area. Above right: a crew of Arab workers lays an asphalt road across the Arabian desert.

Some places look like American towns, with modern air-conditioned houses, schools, hospitals, office buildings, and supermarkets. But right outside such a town, the desert looks very much the way it did hundreds of years ago. Only the miles of pipeline stretching across the desert from oil fields to seaports are new.

The governments of oil-producing countries receive half of the profits, as well as taxes. Jordan, Syria, and Lebanon have no oil wells, but they share in the profits too. The oil companies pay them rent for the right to run their pipelines across these countries.

Because of petroleum, lands which once were very poor have suddenly become rich. Some governments are using part of this money for irrigation, housing, health, roads, and schools. But a large part of the oil wealth remains in the hands of a few rulers, who use it for their own benefit.

This neat community at Dhahran, Saudi Arabia, houses American employees of a large oil company.

Courtesy of TWA—Trans World Airlines

Holy Lands

Southwest Asia was the birthplace of three great world religions: Judaism, Christianity, and Islam. Religion has always played an important part in the history of this region. The greatest number of people in this region are Moslems. That means they are followers of Islam, the religion founded by Mohammed. Most of the people in Turkey, Syria, Jordan, Saudi Arabia, Iraq, and Iran are Moslems. About half of the people in Lebanon are Christians and the majority of the people in Israel are Jews.

Moslems follow the teachings of the Prophet Mohammed, who was born in Mecca in A.D. 570. Their religion plays an important part in their daily lives. Moslems obey the principles of the Koran.

The holy city of Mecca is located near the Red Sea in Saudi Arabia. It is the gathering place of thousands of Moslem pilgrims each year. They come from all over Asia, and from other continents as well.

Courtesy of TWA—Trans World Airlines

Above: As they have done since Biblical days, fishermen still fish the Sea of Galilee.

Below: Jerusalem, sacred to three religions, spreads out below the Mount of Olives.

Courtesy of TWA—Trans World Airlines

Shrines dot the Mount of Olives, where Jesus kept vigil in the Garden of Gethsemane.

Each pilgrim takes part in many religious ceremonies, fasting and praying for nine days. At the end of this time he is entitled to wear a special turban and to call himself "Hajji" (pilgrim). Because Mecca is a holy city, people of other religions are not permitted to enter.

Jerusalem is regarded as a holy city by all three religions. For Jews it is closely tied in with the history of their people as told in the Old Testament.

Christians have always considered it a holy city because it is the scene of so many events in the life of Jesus.

Moslems consider it only a little less holy than Mecca and Medina. They believe that Mohammed, while praying at a holy rock in Jerusalem, was carried off by the Angel Gabriel to visit heaven.

Today, Jerusalem has been divided into two parts. The old city is ruled by Jordan. The new city is the capital of Israel. Jews may not pass through the gates into the old city. Nor may Jordanians pass into modern Jerusalem.

The two sections are entirely different in appearance. New Jerusalem is a modern city. It has wide streets, automobiles, and modern buildings. Most of the people wear modern clothes.

Old Jerusalem contains many of the holy places sacred to Jews, Christians, and Moslems. It is a typical Arab city with narrow, winding streets, open-air bazaars, long-robed Arabs, camels, and donkeys.

In the old city are the ruins of Solomon's Temple. A beautiful Moslem mosque, called the Dome of the Rock, stands inside a walled courtyard called the Haram esh-Sherif. Part of the wall is believed to be the remains of Solomon's Temple. For years devout Jews made pilgrimages to pray at this "Wailing Wall," and to mourn the destruction of the temple. Today Jews are not permitted to enter this part of Jerusalem.

For Christians, old Jerusalem is an equally holy city. Here is the path Jesus followed to Calvary. Here is the Church of the Holy Sepulchre, the site of Jesus' tomb. This church is the place most often visited by Christian pilgrims. Outside the walls of the city are the Gardens of Gethsemane. And still farther on are other holy places on the slopes of the Mount of Olives.

Courtesy of TWA—Trans World Airlines

The Himalayas, the world's highest mountains, form the boundary between India and Tibet.

Houseboats are a familiar sight in Kashmir, a fertile land of many beautiful lakes.

Ewing Krainin—Monkmeyer

SOUTHERN ASIA

Southern Asia juts out from the continent of Asia into the Indian Ocean. In shape it is like a huge triangle. Today there are three main nations in this region: India and Pakistan on the mainland, and the island of Ceylon. All three were once part of the British Empire. Since the end of World War II they have been independent nations. However, they still feel close ties with Great Britain. Therefore they have joined her in the Commonwealth of Nations.

There are also two smaller countries, Bhutan and Nepal. These countries are located in the Himalayas. Because the mountains are very steep, farming is difficult, and not enough food can be raised to support many people. They have been almost completely isolated until recently, because the roughness of the terrain made building roads and railroads too expensive. But a modern road and air service now link Nepal to India. Bhutan may get such connections in the future.

Southern Asia can be divided roughly into three land areas. In the north are the snow-covered Himalayas. South of the mountains are the broad, fertile, hot plains of three great rivers: the Ganges, the Indus,

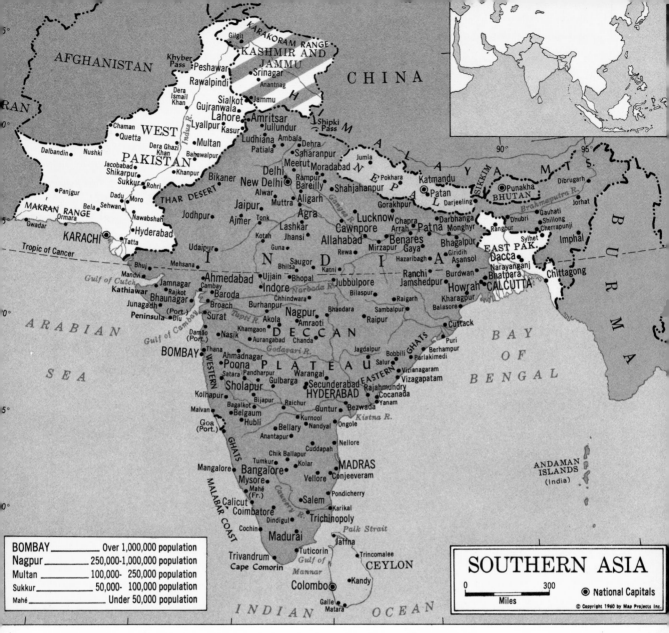

SOUTHERN ASIA

0   300
Miles

◉ National Capitals

© Copyright 1960 by Map Projects Inc.

and the Brahmaputra. The third and main part of the peninsula forms a great plateau, called the Deccan. It is bordered on the east and west by highlands, called *ghats*.

Southern Asia is one of the most densely populated regions in the world. Most of the people live in the river and coastal plains and the deltas. The plains of the three rivers are the most heavily populated. Other densely populated places are the narrow lowlands on the east and west coasts, and in southwest Ceylon. Some places in southern Asia are too mountainous or too dry for people to live.

Most of the Indian peninsula has a tropical climate. It is either hot or very warm all year round. As in many places in Asia, winds called monsoons play an important part in the lives of the people.

The wet monsoons blow from the southwest across the Indian Ocean. From June to October they bring heavy rainfall to many places in southern Asia. The heaviest rain falls where mountains force the winds to rise and drop their moisture. The west coast of India and the plains of the Ganges, Indus, and Brahmaputra rivers receive the heaviest rainfall.

The dry monsoons blow across Asia from the northwest from November to May. They bring the hot, dry season to southern Asia.

Some parts of Asia get little or no rain all year round. The land in West Pakistan which borders Iran and Afghanistan is practically a desert. Few people live there. Most people live where there is plenty of rainfall to raise crops for food.

The varied land and climate in southern Asia support many different kinds of plants, shrubs, trees, flowers, and vines. Over 15,000 different flowering plants have been found in India alone. In the hot, moist lowlands, tropical trees and plants grow in dense monsoon forests. On the slopes of the Himalayas, maple, birch, oak, pine, and other temperate-climate trees are found. The dry areas have thorny scrub forests, bushes, grass, and cactus. Much of India's forest land has been cleared to make way for farms. When farm land loses its fertility and is abandoned, it is quickly overgrown with dense growths of bamboo and other jungle plants.

Many wild and dangerous animals live in the dense tropical jungles of southern Asia. Tigers and leopards prey upon farm animals. Sometimes tigers become man-killers. Wild elephants are still hunted and tamed to do heavy work. The forests, swamps, and jungles are alive with monkeys, wild boars, deer, antelope, wild goats, and even rhinoceros. Poisonous snakes such as the cobra are common. They even invade gardens and houses. Crocodiles live in the rivers, and colorful tropical birds abound in the trees.

Whole families spend long hours in the rice fields hand-harvesting India's important rice crop.

Vidyavrata—FLO

The Ganges, sacred Hindu river, begins its 1,600-mile trip through India high in the Himalayas.

This Calcutta temple was built by Jainists, who refuse to inflict pain on other living creatures.

People of Southern Asia

Southern Asia has a variety of people who differ in appearance, religion, and language. Because of the hundreds of languages and dialects spoken in this part of Asia, English has become the common language spoken by people of wealth and education and in business and government.

Religion divides the people even more than language. The chief religions are Hindu, Moslem, Buddhist, Sikh, Parsee, Jain, and Christian. Hinduism is the chief religion of India.

Hindus believe in many gods. They believe that at death a person's soul passes into the body of another person or an animal. Hindus therefore avoid killing any living thing. Cows are particularly sacred.

As a result Hindus eat no meat. In fact, their religion prevents them from destroying harmful insects and animals which destroy much needed food. In several cities sacred cows and monkeys wander through the streets unharmed by the Hindus.

The Hindu religion separates people into several classes or castes. Brahmans are the highest caste. The lowest are the "untouchables." The caste system makes many strict rules for Hindus to follow. Persons may not marry outside their caste. Many kinds of work are restricted to certain castes. The untouchables are allowed to do only the hardest and most despised kinds of work.

No Hindu may hope to rise above the caste into which he was born. The new Indian Constitution has abolished the castes. But old habits and beliefs are hard to change. The government finds it almost impossible to enforce the new laws.

Buddhism was founded by Gautama Buddha, an Indian prince. It has several beliefs in common with Hinduism. Buddhists believe in the rebirth of souls and that it is wrong to kill living creatures. But they do not have the Hindu caste system.

Sikhism and Jainism are both derived from Hinduism. The Sikhs believe in only one god. They are allowed to eat meat. They were formerly very warlike. Jains believe so strongly in the sacredness of life that they will not even kill insects.

Pakistan and India became separate nations because of religious differences. Pakistan is a Moslem country. The caste system is not followed there.

Ceylon has the greatest number of Buddhists in south Asia. Both in appearance and religion the people of Ceylon are much like the Asians living in the southeast and the far east.

The sacred cows of the Hindus are permitted to roam freely through the streets in India.

Valentina Rosen

Kulwant Roy

A Hindu farmer and his family pose outside their home. Seven out of ten Indians are farmers.

This Sikh, with traditional beard and turban, is a member of India's presidential guard.

Before praying, this Brahmin puts the traditional color mark on his forehead.

A farm woman from northern India displays her favorite piece of jewelry—a nose ring.

Kulwant Roy

Kulwant Roy

Farms and Villages

A farmer in southern Asia raises the same crops and tills the soil in the same way his ancestors did for centuries. He lives in a little village of 100 to 500 families. Often the village is not even on a real road. People who travel must use rutted dirt paths that cross the fields. All the fields lie outside the village.

Farms in southern Asia are usually very small. Few are over five acres. Each farmer inherited his bit of land from his father, who divided the land equally among his sons. Each son will in turn divide his land among his own sons. In this way farms tend to get smaller and smaller as time goes on.

Often a farmer does not own enough land to support his large family. Then he must rent land from a rich landowner. He must work hard from sunrise to sunset in order to grow enough food for his family and to raise money for taxes, rent, and the few necessities he must buy.

The farmer worries about weather just as farmers do all over the world. But he has more worries—floods, drought, hot winds, plant diseases, and plagues of locusts.

Because some of his land is rented, he must often work in widely separated fields. He carries his tools back and forth on his back each morning and night. Sometimes he owns a bullock to pull the old-fashioned wooden plow.

The south Asian farmer understands little about modern farming methods. Nor does he own any modern farm machines. All of his work is done by hand. His sons work in the fields too. Even very young children learn quite early how to help pull weeds.

Because the climate is warm, most farmers are able to grow two crops a year. But they seldom get a very large crop. The land has been worn out from centuries of poor farming methods. The seed which the farmer saves each year to plant his new crops is often of poor quality. Sometimes it carries the germs of plant disease, so that each year's harvest continues to be small.

The farmers have not learned to change the kind of crops which they plant on the same piece of land each year. Most important, the land needs fertilizer. But the farmer does not have money to buy fertilizer. The cow manure which could be used

This humble village near Delhi is typical of many Indian villages. Note the thatched hut.

C. J. Coulson—Shostal

Ferreira—FLO

This boy uses an age-old method of plowing. Children provide India with much of her labor.

Vidyavrata—FLO

The weight of the workers as they run up and down the pole operates this water well.

to enrich the land is dried and used as fuel for cooking. Firewood is scarce.

Sometimes the monsoon winds come late and the crops fail for lack of rain. Sometimes there are floods which wash away the fields. Then the farmer must borrow from the *bania* or moneylender. He pays a high rate of interest. Often the farmer never gets out of debt. If he cannot pay what he owes, the *bania* may take away his land.

After his long day in the field, the farmer and his sons return to their little mud hut with its thatched roof. The house is small and crowded. Married sons bring their wives to live in the family home. The young wives obey their mother-in-law. The father is the head of the household and manages the money for everyone in the family.

The farmer's wife cooks the food and takes care of the household. Like her husband, she follows the ways of her ancestors. Cooking is done on a sheet of cast iron over a tiny fire in the courtyard. Every family eats *chappatis*—a kind of bread, shaped like a pancake, and baked fresh each day. Rice, cereals, and a few vegetables make up the main diet.

There are usually many children in the farmer's family. The little boys take the

cows to pasture or help their fathers in the fields. Little girls help to grind the grain and carry water from the village well. Most villages have a shallow pond where the women come each day to wash clothes and cattle are watered. The village families also get their drinking water there.

India has a great many cattle. Cows wander through the village, into the fields, and even into the houses. Since the Hindu religion forbids eating meat or killing the cattle, they are used only for milk or as work animals.

Indian women are "at home" in the fields. A small sickle is used for harvesting wheat.

Tony Chapelle—Monkmeyer

East Pakistan is a hot, damp lowland. Tropical plants like coconut palms and jute do well here.

There is never enough grass or grain to feed the cattle. Since they may not be killed, they simply die of old age or disease. However, the Indian farmer makes good use of their skins. Cattle hides are an important export item in southern Asia.

Millions of farm families live on the fertile plains of the Ganges River. They raise rice, barley, maize, and oil seeds for food. The river delta, where heavy rains flood the land, is ideal for planting rice. Wheat, barley, and gram are planted in October and harvested in February or March. Rice and millet need heat and water. They are planted in July and harvested in September.

The farmer keeps what he needs to feed his family for the rest of the year. He sells the balance to pay his debts and to buy a few necessary clothes or tools.

Some crops in southern Asia are grown as "money" or "cash" crops. Sugar cane and cotton are grown on millions of acres of land in India. Southern Asia also produces tea, coffee, tobacco, coconuts, rubber, spices, indigo, quinine, and many kinds of fruit. Linseed, peanuts, sesame, and castor beans are important. These oil-producing plants provide money and oil for food.

Most of the world's supply of jute is grown in East Pakistan. Jute is used to make rope and the sacks in which potatoes and sugar are packed. Jute plants grow best in the hot, wet climate of the Ganges and Brahmaputra river deltas.

Workers plant the seeds in spring. When the plants have grown tall, they are cut, tied into bundles, and thrown into pools or creeks to ferment or *ret*. Then the workers can separate the fibers from the stalks. The fiber is baled and shipped to market in ox-carts. Most of the jute fiber is made into rope or sackcloth in Calcutta's many mills.

Some parts of southern Asia are irrigated. The hills in West Pakistan and the plains in western Punjab and Sind use water from the melting snows of the high

Himalaya Mountains. Irrigation water also comes from the monsoon rains that drench the southern slopes of the Himalayas.

Land in West Pakistan is planted in terraces or steps. Water is brought to the terraces by means of dams, canals, and ditches. Deep wells are dug in some places. In these irrigated regions, winter wheat is an important crop. Barley, corn, sorghum, and millet are raised in the summer, often by dry-farming methods.

Like the farmer of India, the Pakistani farmer lives in a little village and goes to his fields each day. However, Pakistanis are Moslems and can eat meat. So they raise cattle, sheep, and goats for food as well as for hides, wool, and milk.

Ceylon, the "Pearl of the Orient," is famous for its tea. Almost all the tea is raised on plantations owned by Europeans.

Tea needs a warm, moist climate. It grows best on the slopes of the hills in southwestern Ceylon. Other important crops in Ceylon are cinnamon, coffee, cinchona for quinine, rubber, rice, coconuts, and vegetables.

Ewing Krainin—Photo Researchers

An elephant pulls a plow in Ceylon. Elephants are the "tractors" of southern Asia.

Ceylonese women pick tea. After picking, the leaves must be "cured" before they are shipped.

Ed Drews—Photo Researchers

Kulwant Roy

Metal windmills, only recently used in Indian irrigation, dot the countryside near Delhi.

C. J. Coulson—Shostal

New sanitary wells, like the one above, have been dug under the supervision of agricultural experts, as seen below.

Tony Chapelle—Monkmeyer

Southern Asia—A Changing Land

There are many signs of change and progress in southern Asia today. Since India and Pakistan became independent republics, they have tried to improve living conditions for their people. Though these countries are chiefly agricultural and grow huge amounts of food, they have never been able to feed their large and growing population.

Today, better farming methods, as well as new ways of making a living, are being introduced. Southern Asia is being helped by a number of United Nations organizations. Some of these are the International Bank for Reconstruction, the Food and Agriculture Organization, and the World Health Organization. Great Britain's "Colombo Plan" and the United States' Point Four Program are also helping southern Asians to better their lives.

These groups help many underdeveloped countries. Technical experts are sent to these countries to help to plan and carry out industrial projects for oil-well drilling, electric power, textile manufacture, transportation, and communications.

Doctors, nurses, specialists in soil chemistry, sanitary engineers, teachers, and other experts have been sent to southern Asia by the United States and other UN countries.

As a result, new factories, new mines, better railroads and roads, improved farming methods, increased crop yields, irrigation projects, power dams, and more schools and hospitals are helping the nations of southern Asia meet their problems. The Soviet Union is also sending experts to the countries of south Asia and helping them to build new dams, roads, and industrial plants.

The Community Development Program is one way in which Indian farmers are being helped. Farm experts are sent into villages. These experts are Indian, too. They speak the language of the people.

The *Gram Sevaks* (helpers of the villages) as they are called, live in the villages for several weeks. They give the farmers new and better kinds of seeds to plant. They explain new and better ways of cultivating the soil, irrigating it, and harvesting the crops. They bring new tools and farm machinery, and teach the farmers how to use them.

They show how health can be improved by better sanitation. They establish new schools. They help the farmers to organize village cooperatives. In this way farmers learn to help each other as well as themselves.

The *Gram Sevak* goes from village to village. He stays only long enough in each

Hundreds of men have been working on the Bhakra Dam project for more than 10 years.

The Bhakra dam will provide a new source of irrigation and hydroelectric power for India.

Education has improved in Pakistan, but many schools still work with inferior materials.

Indian women study hard to prove themselves worthy of their new equality with men.

place to bring about some improvement. Then he moves on to another village.

But change comes slowly in such old lands. It is hard for people to give up their old ways. Many Indian villages have still not been reached by government helpers. In time, farmers in southern Asia will be able to raise much more on their land. With government help, they will make use of land which is now unfit for farming.

New dams are being built in India and Pakistan. These will provide water for irrigation, for generating electricity, and for flood control. Millions of acres in the dry and semi-arid regions of West Pakistan

and India will become fertile farm land. New methods of double-cropping, fertilizing, and year-round irrigation will increase the amount of crops grown in Ceylon, East Pakistan, and India.

Other changes are taking place in southern Asia. Public education is improving. Adults in farm villages are being taught to read and write. About 70 groups of villages in India are receiving special help from the government to improve education for children. In time, other village groups will be given this help. And later, still others.

However, in spite of the great strides being made to build factories and develop mines in southern Asia, many of the goods produced there are still manufactured in small shops and by home industries. At present these craft industries employ more workers and produce more goods than all of southern Asia's large factory industries.

Handwoven cloth production is carried on by six to seven million people in India alone. Rugs, wooden furniture, metal goods, pottery, leatherwork, and jewelry are manufactured by millions of craftsmen in small village workshops.

Pakistan, where almost no factories existed before that country became independent, now has a large cotton textile and jute industry. Like India, Pakistan's government is encouraging foreign investors and is helping to build other industries such as paper manufacture, chemicals, cement, steel, and shipbuilding. Almost no factories are as yet found in Ceylon, Nepal, and Bhutan, except those that process such products as hides and skins, tea, sugar, and rubber.

Exploration for minerals, especially petroleum, iron ore, and coal is going on in India and Pakistan. India has always had rich coal, iron, and limestone deposits. Manganese, mica, chromite, copper, and bauxite are also mined. India has long been famous for its precious stones. However, mining engineers are discovering new

Joe Barnell—Shostal

Despite modernization, evidenced by the Jamshedpur steel works, age-old customs still prevail.

mineral deposits. Both India and Pakistan are encouraging the search.

Under India's "Five Year Plans," the government is encouraging new industry. Investors from foreign countries have been urged to help develop the mineral resources and to build new factories. The Indian government has also contributed money for industrial development.

Cotton and jute textile mills have long been important in India. Today, Pakistan is also manufacturing these textiles.

Iron and steel production has been important in India for many years. The Tata Steel Works in Jamshedpur are among the largest in Asia. Other factories nearby use the steel to manufacture wire, nails, locomotives, bicycles, ships, and tools.

Handmade clay bricks are still a common building material over a large part of India.

Vidyavrata—FLO

Textiles are one of India's greatest industries, yet much weaving is done with handlooms.

Vidyavrata—FLO

Herbert Knapp

Fields of rice, Asia's chief food crop, stretch for miles across the fertile lowlands of Thailand.

SOUTHEAST ASIA

The southeast corner of Asia is a long peninsula, lying between China and India. On this peninsula are Indochina, Burma, Malaya, and Thailand. The part that was once called Indochina is now made up of several new countries—Laos, Cambodia, and North and South Vietnam. For many years much of southeast Asia belonged to England and France. Since World War II, lands which were once European colonies have become independent nations.

Of the many different kinds of people who live in southeast Asia, there are Burmese, Thais, Malays, Annamese, Cambodians, Shans, Chins, Karens, Kachins, Indians, and Chinese. Many different languages are spoken. Even within a single country, people in neighboring villages may speak very different dialects. There are many different religions, too, but most of the people are Buddhists.

Buddhist monasteries and temples are found throughout southeast Asia. The beautiful Temple of the Emerald Buddha in Bangkok, Thailand, is famous all over the world. Like all Buddhist temples it is surrounded by many tall and brightly colored pagodas. The temples and pagodas are decorated with hundreds of little bells which tinkle musically when the wind blows. There is usually a huge stone statue of Buddha outside the temple or monastery. Sometimes there is even a solid gold Buddha. The courtyard of the temple is beautiful, with tropical plants, flowers, and little pools in which lotus plants and water lilies grow.

J. C. Burke—Photo Library

The sun bounces off the brilliant gold-leaf-covered Buddhist temples, in Rangoon, Burma.

Buddhist monks live in the monasteries. They spend their lives in prayer, teaching, and service to the people. Yellow-robed monks are a common sight all over southeast Asia. Each monk has a shaven head. He carries a wooden begging bowl in which people place gifts of food or money. Often he carries books too, because study and teaching are part of his duties.

A passer-by drops some money into the begging-bowl of a Buddhist monk, who lives on such charity.

Kofod—Monkmeyer

Southeastern Asia is within the tropics. But, because there are a number of mountain ranges stretching southward from the Himalayas, there is a wide variety of climates. The low coastal plains and the river valleys are hot and wet. Tropical plants and trees flourish in such a climate. There are many kinds of palms including coco, nipa, and rattan. Valuable timber trees include teak, ebony, and rosewood. There are mulberry trees, whose leaves are fed to silkworms. Bamboo forests grow on the higher, drier grounds.

Bamboo is actually a grass, not a tree. But it grows to treelike height. Bamboo is one of southeast Asia's most useful plants. The hard, hollow, woody stems are used for building, furniture, water pipes, containers, and drinking cups. The young shoots can be eaten. Bamboo is an especially valuable building material in hot, damp regions because it resists insects and does

Thomas d'Hoste—Shostal

Southeast Asia's chief beast of burden, the water buffalo, is a playmate for this Thai boy.

Margaret Lang—Shostal

This Malayan hut is built on stilts as a protection against floods and wild animals.

not decay easily in this sort of climate.

In the jungles there are tigers, elephants, rhinoceros, leopards, and monkeys. There are tropical birds and many snakes. And the rivers are full of a variety of food fish.

These fish supply a large part of the protein diet for millions of people who live near the rivers. Some native farmers have "fish farms." They raise fish in little ponds near their houses.

Teak logs float down a Thai river from the highlands to the coast, where they will be processed.

A. Kolb, Hamburg

H. Verstappen

Rice—Asia's Staff of Life

Rice is the staff of life for most Asian people. It is as important to children in southeast Asia as bread is to American boys and girls. Most people in southeast Asia eat rice in some form three times a day. The average person there eats from 300 to 400 pounds of rice a year. In the United States the average is only about 6 pounds.

Rice must be sown, transplanted, cultivated, and harvested by hand—a laborious process.

Rice is a cereal grass that grows best where the temperature is high and the soil very wet. It needs a long hot summer. Plenty of water is also needed to flood the fields all during the growing season. Southeast Asia has perfect conditions for growing rice. Much more rice is raised than the people need. Millions of bushels are exported each year to other parts of Asia.

In the delta lands of rivers like the Irrawaddy, rice is planted as soon as the summer monsoon rains flood the land. The rice seeds are scattered directly on the wet, mushy, flooded fields. Rice fields are separated by low dirt walls called dikes or levees, which keep the water from draining away. Each flooded field is called a paddy.

In the drier upland regions, rice fields are sometimes built on the terraced slopes of hills. Rims of sod hold the water in the paddy fields and keep the soil from washing away. Water is brought from nearby rivers through irrigation ditches.

In contrast to the delta lands, seed for irrigated fields is first planted in small, well-fertilized, flooded nursery fields. When the rice plants are several inches tall, they are carefully transplanted.

As the plants grow, more water is added until it is about 6 inches deep. Rice plants grow several feet tall. When the plants begin to ripen, the fields are drained. Farmers use knives or sickles to harvest the rice. The stalks are cut and tied in bundles or sheaves. Then the sheaves are left to dry.

Most rice is threshed by hand. Farmers beat the bundles of rice-stalks against wooden boxes or slotted frames. Sometimes they use a wire screen to sift the rice grains. Sometimes men or animals trample on the sheaves to separate the rice from the stalks.

Rice that has not been cleaned and polished is called paddy. The grains are covered with a hard brown shell or hull. Most farmers clean the paddy by crude home

Fujihira—Monkmeyer

This crude water-scoop makes the task of hand irrigation somewhat easier.

Fujihira—Monkmeyer

A Vietnamese beats bundles of rice stalks against a frame to separate grain from straw.

methods. They pound the rice in a mortar to rub off the hulls. Sometimes they use a hand-operated wooden mill. Often the paddy is shipped to large mills to be hulled and polished. Finally the cleaned rice is packed in sacks for shipment.

Some parts of Asia can grow two crops of rice a year. During the rainy season, "wet rice" is grown. During the dry season, the fields are irrigated. In most places, after the rice fields are cut and drained, farm cattle graze in the fields.

Rice paddies must be plowed to stir up the mud before the seeds are planted.

Fujihira—Monkmeyer

Jerome W. Belford—House of Photography

Latex from Malayan rubber plantations is shipped to all parts of the world.

Ewing Krainin—Photo Researchers

A worker shaves off some of the bark from a rubber tree to permit the latex to seep out.

Rubber and Tin

The Malay Peninsula of southeast Asia produces almost two fifths of the world's rubber. Rubber plantations stretch in a continuous line from Singapore to Penang along the west coast of Malaya. Here the land is low and level and the climate hot and rainy.

Rubber trees were once found only in the New World. An English scientist care-

Sheets of crude rubber—latex coagulated by adding acid—are dried on heavy racks.

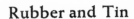

Margaret Lang—Shostal

fully collected thousands of seeds and planted them in the warm greenhouses of a British botanical garden. About 1876, the young plants were shipped to British possessions in southeast Asia. They were planted in Malaya, Ceylon, and the islands of southeast Asia.

Young rubber trees are first grown in a nursery. Later they are transplanted in long straight rows on estates and plantations. Trees are set out in the rainy season—about 150 to an acre. Rubber trees grow quickly, six to nine feet a year.

When a tree is six years old, it is ready to be tapped. Rubber trees produce a milky liquid called latex. A worker shaves off a thin, narrow strip of bark, about a quarter of an inch deep. He makes this cut in a slanting line about four feet above the ground and half way around the tree. The latex drips down the slanting cut through a spout into a little cup.

Every three or four hours the latex is collected in pails and carried to the factory. Trees are usually tapped every other day. Each time the worker makes another narrow cut just below the last one. When these cuts reach within one foot of the ground, the other side of the tree is tapped. Then the bark on the first side gets a chance to grow again. In this way most rubber trees can be tapped for 25 years. Some of the best quality trees give up to 30 pounds of latex a year.

The liquid latex is carried to the factory. There an acid is added and the liquid coagulates or thickens into crude rubber. Now it can be handled. The crude rubber is pressed through rollers into thick sheets, which are carefully dried, folded, and pressed into bales weighing 200 to 250 pounds.

The bales are sent to seaports and shipped all over the world. In the United States raw rubber is manufactured into thousands of useful articles from rubber tires to footwear for snow and rain.

Tin is the most important mineral product of Malaya. One third of the world's tin is mined there. Most of the tin mines are along the west coast, in sand and gravel deposits in river beds. Strong jets of water wash the soil up from the river bottom. A motor carries it in an endless stream to the top of a runway, where it pours down a series of steps. Each step separates some of the tin from the sand, clay, and gravel.

The tin concentrate is taken to the smelters, where it is refined and shaped into ingots. These are sent to seaports such as Penang and Singapore. From there the tin is shipped to users all over the world.

A majority of the tin mines are owned by European or Chinese companies. Most of the workers are Chinese. Tin mining has caused serious problems in Malaya. Great stretches of useless eroded land were left by hydraulic mining. Waste material from the tin refineries was dumped into the rivers and carried downstream, filling up channels and ruining rice paddies. Today the government limits dumping. Tin is an asset to Malaya. But the mines are fast being used up. It is estimated that by 1980 the tin mines will be closed.

The Hong Fatt tin mine, more than 400 feet deep, is one of Malaya's largest mines.

British Information Service

The canals of Thailand are crowded with floating markets, from which sampan dwellers buy supplies.

Life in Southeast Asia

The way people live is almost always related to the land and the climate. This is especially true in southeast Asia, a land of many rivers. The rivers are separated by ranges of mountains and hills, which are often covered by dense tropical rainforests. Overland travel is almost impossible. Most of the people live in the lowlands, in little villages built along the banks of rivers.

Most river villages look very much alike. The houses are built on tall stilts to keep them well above the water level in time of flood. During the rainy season the rivers often rise several feet and lap the floors of the houses. The stilts also protect the family from wild animals.

The tiny houses are made of bamboo, rattan, and thatch. Sometimes the village farmer keeps a few chickens, a pig, or a water buffalo under the floor of the house.

The rivers abound in fish, and the villagers depend greatly on fish for food. Often a farmer builds a little pond near the river and raises his own food fish.

Rivers are the main means of travel, not only for the village people but for the people in coastal cities as well. Steamers travel hundreds of miles up the rivers, carrying passengers, mail, and goods. Sacks of paddy are shipped to coastal mills. Small delivery boats, sampans, and water taxis go where the large steamers cannot.

If you visited this part of Asia you would not call a taxi; instead you would hire a boat or water taxi. Even in big cities like Bangkok, most people travel back and forth to work by water taxi. Many of the cities are criss-crossed by canals which help to drain off water during the monsoons.

The rivers are used to float huge rafts of teak logs from the forests to the coast. Teak grows in tropical hill forests where the climate is hot and rainy. Burma is famous for its teak forests. The wood is valuable for shipbuilding, for fine furniture, and cabinet work.

Teakwood is beautiful when carved and polished. It lasts for hundreds of years without rotting, splitting or warping. Insects cannot harm it. The huge teak logs are hauled to the rivers by elephants. Because green teakwood does not float, the logs are either dried for a year or tied to rafts and sent floating down the rivers.

Many primitive people live deep in the forests and hills. Sometimes they have no permanent homes, but build shelters of branches. These tribes live by hunting, fishing, and gathering roots, nuts, and fruits.

Some of the less primitive tribes live in semipermanent villages and carry on a crude kind of farming. They burn down trees to make a little clearing in the forest. Then they plant seeds by poking holes in the soil with a stick.

In a few years the soil loses its fertility. Then the people move on to another place in the forest, where they clear a little land in the same way.

This mother and her son are typical of the handsome tribesmen from the mountains of Vietnam.

Herbert Knapp

Many people in Thailand live on sampans. Here, a family is about to have its main meal.

Herbert Knapp

Teak logs, which must be dried by the sun before they can float downstream, are put in piles.

Fujihira—Monkmeyer

INTERIOR ASIA

Interior, or central, Asia includes Tibet, Sinkiang, and Mongolia. This is a region of great size and few people. It is a region of mountains, plateaus, and deserts.

Some of Asia's highest mountains, loftiest plateaus, and largest deserts are found here. The Tien Shan and Altai Mountains wall in the region in the north. The Kunluns cut across it, separating Tibet from Sinkiang. In the west rise the Pamirs. The Himalayas in the south separate interior Asia from India.

Two vast deserts — the Gobi and the Takla Makan—occupy hundreds of thousands of square miles. Mountains, deserts, and plateaus fence in this region from the rest of Asia. Interior Asia is far from the oceans with their moderating, rain-bearing winds. Knowing these facts, you can tell much about life in interior Asia.

Tibet is the highest country in the world. Some of its mountain peaks tower over four miles high. The Tibetan plateau itself is as much as three miles above sea level.

Few people can live in this high, cold, mountainous land. Those who do are almost cut off from the rest of Asia. There are no railroads. A narrow, rocky caravan route winds its way through the Himalayas to India.

Another old caravan road, the Tea Road, led to China.

In recent years, Communist China has built two highways leading to the capital city of Lhasa. Thousands of Chinese have used these roads to migrate to Tibet. However, even today most of Tibet's goods are carried on the backs of yaks and mountain ponies.

Most of the people live in the southern part of Tibet. Here the melting snows feed rivers which irrigate the soil. Tibetans have learned how to live in this harsh land. They make the most of their animals. Hides and skins furnish clothing and shelter. The

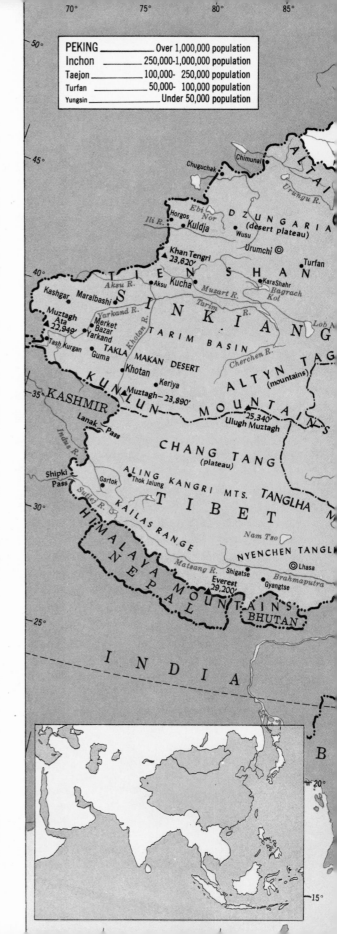

PEKING _____ Over 1,000,000 population
Inchon _____ 250,000-1,000,000 population
Taejon _____ 100,000- 250,000 population
Turfan _____ 50,000- 100,000 population
Yungsin _____ Under 50,000 population

The Potala, in Lhasa, is 400 feet high and 1200 feet long. It is the most important monastery in Tibet, for it is the traditional residence of the Dalai Lama, the head of the Tibetan religion.

meat and milk are food. The animal dung or manure is dried and used for fuel. The bones are made into tools.

Wheat and barley are raised by dry farming methods in small scattered sections. Tsamba, a flour made of roasted wheat or barley, is a common food. Tibetans eat it mixed with butter and hot tea as a kind of cereal. The pastures on the rolling plateaus and mountain slopes are used to raise sheep, cattle, and the strong Tibetan ponies. Yaks, accustomed to high altitudes, pull the plows and serve as pack animals.

The religion of most Tibetans is Lamaism, a kind of Buddhism. Thousands of young boys are placed in monasteries where they study for years. They become Buddhist monks, or lamas. The Dalai Lama has been the traditional leader of the Tibetan people.

Sinkiang (Chinese Turkestan) is a high plateau bordered by still higher mountains.

On ceremonial days, Tibetan lamas march in processions. This temple is a starting point.

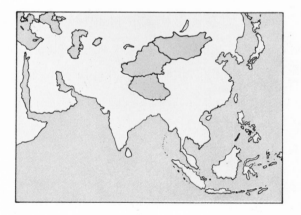

Colin Wyatt—Photo Researchers

George Holton—Photo Library

This expedition, in search of the "abominable snow-man" of the Himalayas, camps at 15,000 feet.

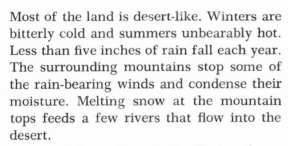

George Holton—Photo Library

The Sherpa tribe lives in the mountains. They are used to high altitudes and make good guides.

Most of the land is desert-like. Winters are bitterly cold and summers unbearably hot. Less than five inches of rain fall each year. The surrounding mountains stop some of the rain-bearing winds and condense their moisture. Melting snow at the mountain tops feeds a few rivers that flow into the desert.

One of these rivers is the Tarim. Oases border the foothills of the mountains near the Tarim River. Food crops, especially wheat, can be raised. There is enough mois-

ture in the surrounding land to grow grass. Nomadic herdsmen raise sheep and cattle. They come to the oasis villages to trade wool, hides, meat, butter, and cheese for grain, leather, cloth, and tea.

Mongolia lies high among the mountains of interior Asia. Most of the land is a vast, rolling plateau over 3,000 feet high. Part of Mongolia is in the great Gobi Desert, where explorers have discovered the remains of many prehistoric animals.

In the 13th century Genghis Khan and his Mongol tribes overran and conquered all of Asia from the Pacific to the Black Sea. His grandson, Kublai Khan, was visited by the great Venetian traveler Marco Polo. He brought back to Europe tales of the wonders of "far Cathay."

Most of the plateau region in Mongolia is covered with grass. Nomadic tribes travel from place to place with their herds of

Eastfoto

An oasis in Sinkiang is a pleasant contrast to the surrounding mountainous country.

Ergy Landau—Rapho Guillumette

Towns in Outer Mongolia are small. This desolate country is inhabited primarily by nomads.

sheep, goats, camels, and horses. To a Mongol, his herds are the most important thing in life.

From his flocks he gets food—meat, butter, milk, and cheese. The sheepskin gives him clothing and hides. The wool is made into felt for his boots, his bedding, and his round tent, or *yurt*. The dried dung of animals is gathered for fuel.

His horses, camels, and yaks furnish transportation. Except for tea, which is imported from China, and tsamba from Tibet, the Mongol tribesman gets everything he needs from his flocks.

The Mongol tribesman looks down upon farmers, who must stay in one place to tend their fields. The Mongol prefers to ride on the back of his horse or camel, tending his flocks. When the grass in one place is gone, he moves his flocks, his yurts, his few household belongings, and his family to new pastures.

The Mongol yurt is a round, dome-shaped hut made of heavy cloth, woven from the wool of sheep and goats. The felt cloth is stretched over a collapsible frame made of wooden poles. Though light in weight, these yurts are strong and furnish fine protection against the worst blizzards. In addition they can be taken down easily and carried from place to place when the Mongol tribe must move its flocks.

In winter the livestock often suffers from lack of food. Freezing blizzards sometimes form hard ice-crusts over the snows; so the animals are unable to get at the dried grass underneath. In recent years the government has built thousands of covered sheds and shelters to protect livestock during storms and severe cold. But most tribes protect their herds by building open winter camps. Corrals are built, similar to those in the western part of the United States, to protect the animals from cold winter winds and from wolves. The corral walls are made of bricks of animal dung. Dung "chips"—like the buffalo "chips" of the early American west—are gathered and burned directly as fuel. They are the most available fuel.

A Mongol tribesman leads a nomadic life. His yurt, or portable home, is made of wool felt.

A family group in Outer Mongolia. They are Buddhists and speak the Mongol tongue.

Many flocks must still be wintered on the open range. The 13,000 wolf skins taken each year indicate the number of wolves which prey on the livestock, especially sheep. In recent years some hay has been raised. This has helped cut the deaths of livestock from starvation.

Today, both Soviet Russia and China (Chinese People's Republic) are making great attempts to influence Mongolia (Mongolian People's Republic). Mongolia is not only a "buffer" separating the two great Communist powers, but is a possible source of rich mineral wealth still undiscovered.

Because they depend on their flocks, the life of many Mongols is a continual search for pastures.

Ergy Landau—Rapho Guillumette

EASTERN ASIA

For thousands of years the countries of eastern Asia kept to their own way of life. For centuries this part of Asia was closed to the outside world.

China is shut in on the west, north, and south by high mountains, plateaus, or deserts. On the east, the Pacific Ocean is a barrier thousands of miles wide. Man could not cross it easily.

China, the largest country in eastern Asia, is one of the oldest in the world. Man

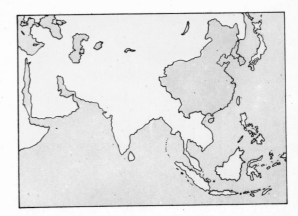

Roads in remote parts of China are apt to be no more than winding foot paths.

A. Mayer

has probably lived there over a longer period of time than any other place on earth. Scientists say that a human skull discovered near Peking is probably half a million years old.

We know that thousands of years ago the Chinese had developed a high civilization. They invented paper, printing, gunpowder, porcelain, and silk weaving.

Except for early explorers like Marco Polo, or the caravan traders who brought silk across the immense continent of Asia, few Europeans had ever visited there. Only a few people knew much about China and the other countries of eastern Asia before the end of the nineteenth century. Today China is under Communist control. The western world still knows less about China than about many other places in Asia.

However, we do know a great deal about the land and the climate of eastern Asia. We know about the many different landforms in China. The provinces of Tibet and Sinkiang have some of the world's highest mountains, and the Takla Makan Desert is one of the driest places on earth. We know that millions of acres of land in interior Asia and western China are almost useless to man.

But China contains some of the best land in the world too. The fertile river valleys and coastal plains are among the most densely populated places in the world.

The soil in the river valleys has been worked over for so many hundreds, even thousands, of years that it is probably very

The Great Wall of China was built in the third century B.C. as a defense against Mongol invaders.

different from what it once was. Every inch of land is made to grow the greatest amount of food possible. China's steadily growing population makes food production a constant problem.

Many great rivers rise in the mountains of western China. They flow through steep-sided gorges and through fertile valleys to empty at last into the China Sea and the Pacific Ocean.

For thousands of years these great rivers have carved their valleys and built up broad, fertile plains. For thousands of years the melting snows in the mountains and the heavy monsoon rains have made the rivers overflow their banks and flood the land.

Sometimes these floods cause great destruction. Thousands of years ago the Chinese were already building dikes and canals to control the flood waters and to irrigate the land. Today China's coastal plains are criss-crossed with a network of canals and rivers. Thousands of peasants live on river-boats tied to the banks of these waterways.

China is the world's largest rice producer. The grain which feeds her people is raised in paddies.

Farming in China

Farming is the way of life for four fifths of China's people. But in China there has never been enough good land to go around. For thousands of years every Chinese family has wanted to own its own piece of land.

As time went on, most of the good land fell into the hands of a few wealthy landowners. By 1945 more than half the Chinese farmers were tenants working on land they did not own and for which they had to pay heavy taxes and large rents.

Often a Chinese farm family continued to till the same piece of land for hundreds of years. But the poor peasant could never hope to earn enough to feed his family or pay for his own land.

One of China's most fruitful farming regions is the delta of the Si Kiang (Si River). The Si is in southern China. It flows past the city of Canton and empties into the South China Sea near Hong Kong.

The climate of the Si River delta is subtropical. The long, hot summer months bring heavy monsoon rains, and there is never any frost. Tea, sweet potatoes, mulberry trees for silk production, and a great variety of semi-tropical fruits and vegetables are grown. But the chief crop is rice. The long growing season allows at least two crops of rice a year.

For the last fifty centuries the Chinese farmers have learned how to get the most out of their land. They know rice produces more food per acre than any other crop.

The Chinese farmer, his sons, and his wife all work in the fields. They plant rice, pump water into the paddy fields, cultivate, and harvest the plants by hand. Once in a while some farmer owns a buffalo which is used for plowing. But most farmers do all the work themselves.

Farmers live in little villages made up of a cluster of farmhouses. Houses are usually made of mud-and-bamboo walls with a thatched roof. The floor is made of hard-packed earth. A whole family—grandparents, parents, and children live in a little group of houses built around a family courtyard.

Under the Chinese Communist government, large landowners were forced to give up their land. Small farms, seldom more than three acres, were then distributed to the peasants. Even so, the population was so large that there was still not enough land for each farmer to feed his family properly. If there was a poor crop, or a flood, thousands of peasants were in danger of starvation.

In an attempt to increase food production, the government has now organized the small farms into large state-run farms, called communes. Each peasant pools his land and tools with that of other farmers and, in turn, is supposed to receive his food and clothing from the government.

Large farm machines have been introduced in some communes. As a result the old-fashioned Chinese farm landscape with its tiny fields is fast disappearing. However, many Chinese farmers find the change from their old ways of family farming hard to accept. The government has found a good deal of resistance to the communes.

The life of a Chinese farmer is hard. It will take time before machines are widespread.

John Strohm

Most Chinese must do all their work by hand. The tools which are available are very primitive.

The farmer who owns a water buffalo is lucky indeed. The animal can be used to help plow.

Heavy use of fertilizer, spread by hand, has kept the soil of southern China fertile for centuries.

These Chinese boys are pictured with oxen. But animals are not common on Chinese farms.

A Chinese farmer winnows grain. He is separating the good grain from the chaff.

Farmers on a commune near Peking. Many Chinese prefer the old system of private farms.

Sampans are widely used as year-round residences in the overcrowded river cities of China.

People of the Sampan

Millions of people in southeast China live and work all their lives on rivers and canals. No other region in the world has such a network of navigable waterways. In addition to the rivers, there are thousands of miles of canals. In this part of China waterways take the place of roads.

Every village, town, and city is on a river or canal. Many of the larger cities are hundreds of miles inland on China's great rivers. Canals often criss-cross these cities. Boats are used instead of cars, trucks, or trains to carry goods and people.

Chinese boats are called junks and sampans. They come in all sizes and have changed little in thousands of years. Some are very small and carry only a few people and a little cargo. Others are large enough to carry enormous cargoes up and down the coast and out to sea.

Some boats are used to ferry people from place to place in cities like Canton and Hong Kong. Many more are used as homes for the hundreds of thousands of people who can find no room on the land.

Many junks are used for fishing. Chinese fishermen go out to sea to catch fish, shrimps, and oysters and to find edible seaweed. Fish is an important food in China.

Some junks are used as ferries. Although they look awkward, they are very seaworthy.

A sampan on a Chinese river is home to this family. They eat, sleep, and live on board.

Ruth V. Bair

Even the river people who live on houseboats, or sampans, fish in the inland lakes, canals, and rivers. Sometimes the fishermen use cormorants which they have trained to catch fish.

Cormorants, which resemble seagulls, are fine divers. The fisherman ties a string to the bird's leg and a noose of straw rope around its neck. When the bird dives for a fish, the fisherman pulls on the straw noose to keep the bird from swallowing the fish. Then the bird is hauled into the boat and the fish is removed from its bill.

Some riverboat dwellers live all their lives on board their boats. Sometimes the sampans are tied up to the shore. Often a boat is tied to other boats far from land. Small children and the family's chickens may be tied to the deck to keep from falling into the water. Sometimes families grow small plants and vegetables on board their boats. In Canton more than one tenth of the people live on the rivers and canals. In Hong Kong alone 100,000 Chinese live aboard boats.

Some boats on the Yangtze River near Shanghai are houseboats. Others are commercial vessels.

Camera Clix

John Strohm

The Ming Tombs dam project will provide hydroelectric power for the Peking area.

China's Industrial Northland

The Hwang Ho, or Yellow River, of north China flows through the great north China plains. For thousands of years this river and its many branches have carried the fertile yellow mud from the inland "loess" plateau, and spread it over the north China plains.

Loess soil is very fertile. It can produce rich crops of millet, wheat, soybeans, peanuts, sesame, and kaoliang (sorghum) if there is enough rainfall.

But in some years there are severe droughts in north China. The crops fail and there is famine. At other times there is too much rain. Then the Hwang Ho floods and bursts through its dikes. As a result, thousands of people are drowned or die of starvation.

China once had many beautiful forests. Long ago the people cut down the trees and did not plant new ones. Today there are few forests and very little wood for building or for fuel. Most of the land in the heavily populated regions is bare of trees. Only on

Most of the construction of the Ming Tombs dam has been done by men, rather than by machines.

John Strohm

Many women are laborers in Manchuria. Here we see one at work in a busy cable factory.

John Strohm

the mountain slopes of north China are there any large forests today.

The loss of China's forests is the reason for the soil erosion. The forests kept rain from washing good soil away. The endless miles of deep, barren gulleys and massive bluffs which are a common sight on China's landscape were caused by the destruction of forests centuries ago.

Manchuria in northeast China is a region very much like our north central plains states. There are rolling, grassy prairies and forest-covered mountains bordering the plains. Dry, icy winds blow out of Siberia in the winter, but the summers are warm and moist. The summer monsoon that blows from the ocean brings rain in July and August.

Communist China's most modern "state farms" are in Manchuria, where the land is suitable for large-scale farming with machinery. But as recently as 1956 only one hundredth of Manchuria's farmland was cultivated by machinery.

Manchuria contains some of China's most important heavy industries. There are vast iron reserves as well as large deposits of coal, magnesite, and aluminum. Valuable iron and coal mines are located near each other. Because fuel and ore are close together, such nearby cities as Mukden (Shenyang) and Anchang (An-shan) have built up important steel mills and metal industries.

Manchuria has better railroads than any other part of China. The railway lines were originally built by the Russians and later taken over by the Japanese. Manchuria's railroads tie in with those of Korea and Siberia as well as those of China.

Before World War II the Japanese had developed hydroelectric power plants, iron and steel works, chemical, aluminum, rubber, and food-processing factories as well as munitions works. Today, the Chinese Communist government, with the help of Russian technicians, is continuing to expand north China's industries.

John Strohm

Another long day's work begins in this productive steel mill in Anchang, Manchuria.

John Strohm

An aerial view shows the years of work that have gone into this large open-pit coal mine.

Oil tanks in the Yumen oilfields dot the Gobi desert, China's new industrial frontier.

Eastfoto

Hamilton Wright Organization, Inc.

Fishing is important to the economy of Formosa. This is a good catch off the coast at NanFanAo.

Formosa

The island of Formosa (Taiwan) lies 100 miles off the coast of south China. It is the stronghold of the Chinese Nationalist government. Before World War II, China was torn by wars with Japan, as well as by years of civil war between government troops, Communists, and bandit gangs.

After World War II, civil war continued between the Chinese Communists under Mao Tse-tung and the Chinese Nationalists under Chiang Kai-shek. In 1949 the Communists succeeded in defeating the Nationalists, who were then forced to flee from the mainland. Chiang moved his army and set up his government on Formosa.

Formosa is part of the chain of western Pacific volcanic islands which includes the islands of Japan. Formosa is only about 235 miles long and 90 miles at its widest. This is roughly one third the size of Cuba.

Less than one fourth of the land is usable for farming. Most of the central part is a giant mountain range which runs the length of the island from north to south. Forty-eight peaks are over 10,000 feet high.

On the east coast the mountains descend steeply right down to the Pacific Ocean. The narrow western coastal plain is less than 25 miles wide in most places.

Formosa's climate varies with the prevailing winds. During the summer, southwest winds bring heavy rains to the south and west coastal plains. Then the northern part of the island is clear and dry.

From October through March the northeast winds blow, bringing heavy rains to the northern and eastern parts of the island, while the south and west are clear.

Sometimes during the late summer fierce typhoons bring destruction to homes, farms, and villages. Torrents of rain cause the mountain streams to flood, sometimes burying fertile fields under tons of stones, gravel, and sand.

About nine tenths of Formosa's inhabitants are Chinese. However, the original Formosans were not Chinese, but primitive, brown-skinned Malays. Until recent years some of these tribes still practiced headhunting. Today only about 200,000 of them are left. They live in the hilly part of the island, while the fertile lowlands have been taken over by the Chinese.

Japan controlled the island from 1895 to 1945. During those years Japan developed Formosa's industry, built railroads, factories, and hydroelectric plants. The island supplied Japan with large amounts of rice and sugar.

Today there are about 10 million people, mostly Chinese, living on the island of Formosa. Many of these inhabitants fled from the mainland of China with Chiang Kai-shek's Nationalist government. Some live in cities like Taipei, the capital. Many more live in little farm villages surrounded by rice paddies.

In city or village, the Chinese live the way they did on the mainland. They carry on the same kind of work, the same cus-

Chinese Nationalist soldiers are reviewed by offi-cers at a recruit training center at Taichung.

Because of its growing textile industry, more flax is being cultivated on Formosa.

toms and habits. Rice is the chief crop. More than half the land is given over to rice paddies. Sugar cane is important too. Formosa also raises sweet potatoes, tropical fruits, jute, soybeans, and peanuts.

There are many small factories. They make textiles, chemicals, ceramics, ma-chinery, and processed foods. Sugar refin-ing is the most important industry

Formosa's forests are valuable too. More than two thirds of the island is covered with forests. Three fourths of the world's supply of camphor comes from Formosa's cam-phor trees.

Sugar cane is an important crop. Here it is harvested by a roadside in southwest Taiwan.

Thomas Benner—Shostal

A Korean village sits at the base of barren hills. Deforestation has ruined much land in Korea.

Korea

The peninsula of Korea juts out from the mainland toward the islands of Japan. It is separated from Japan by the Sea of Japan, from China by the Yellow Sea, and from Manchuria and the U.S.S.R. by the Yalu and Tumen rivers.

Korea is a land of many mountains. Only about one fifth of the land is level and fertile enough for farming. Fertile land borders the coast, and many of the narrow valleys between the hills can be cultivated.

North and South Korea differ in many ways. The mountains in North Korea are higher, more rugged and heavily forested. The climate is more severe, with colder winters. In spite of this, North Korea is more highly industrialized. The Japanese, who controlled Korea before World War II, built factories, railroads, and hydroelectric plants there.

South Korea is more agricultural. The climate is warmer and the winters are quite mild. Rice is the chief crop on the coastal lowlands. After the rice is harvested, the fields are drained and planted to barley, cotton, wheat, and other crops. But the surrounding hills and mountains are almost bare of trees and vegetation. As in many

Korean farmers carry huge loads of rice on their backs from the fields to the threshing floor.

Ewing Galloway

These vegetables, chopped up and pickled, will become kimchi, Korea's national dish.

Sanford Gorby—Shostal

parts of China, the destruction of Korea's forests centuries ago has caused serious soil erosion.

South Korea is densely populated. A large proportion of its 21 million people live in the farm villages along the crowded coastal plains. Korean houses are shaped like the letter "L" or "U." Each house is surrounded by a wall.

Most of the Korean family life is centered in the courtyards of the houses. Here the rice is dried and threshed. Here the women make "kimchi"—a mixture of pickled radishes and spices, Korea's national dish. Clothes are washed and dried in the yard.

Each courtyard has its little vegetable garden and some fruit trees. On the level ground outside the village, rice is grown. On the higher slopes, upland crops are raised—wheat, barley, millet, rye, buckwheat, and vegetables.

Old people are greatly honored in Korea. They dress in white—the color of most Korean clothes. They often have long whiskers. On their heads they wear tall black hats made of horsehair.

Korea is a land divided by war. After World War II, Korea was taken from Japan. Russian troops occupied the northern part and American troops the south. When the government of the Republic of Korea was

Edmund N. Paige—Shostal

This old gentleman wears the traditional black horsehair hat and white clothing of Korea.

organized, the United States withdrew its troops. In 1950 Communists from North Korea invaded the South Korean republic.

The Korean War caused great damage to South Korea. Millions of people were left homeless. Almost half a million homes were destroyed. Industries and transportation facilities were hard hit, and villages near the battle line were destroyed. Since the end of the Korean War, many United Nations agencies have been helping South Korea get back on her feet.

Traditional tile-roofed houses contrast with American jeeps in Seoul, South Korea's capital.

Ewing Krainin—Photo Researchers

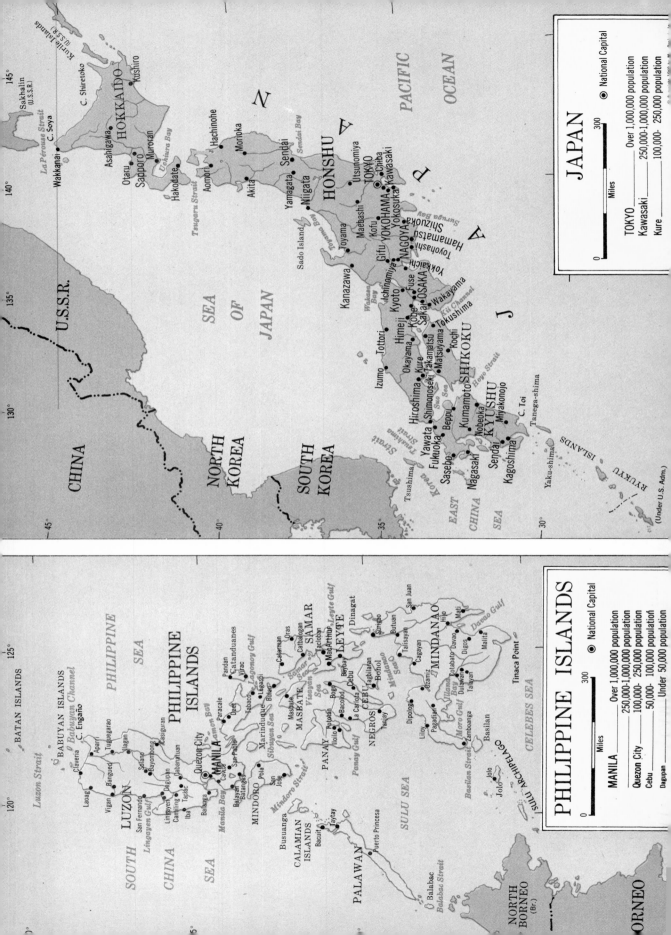

REPUBLIC OF INDONESIA

◉ National Capital

© Copyright 1960 by Map Projects Inc.

JAKARTA	Over 1,000,000 population
Bandung	250,000–1,000,000 population
Banjermasin	100,000– 250,000 population
Pasuruan	50,000– 100,000 population
Sintang	Under 50,000 population

Miles
0   300

Nagasaki, a leading Japanese port, was the first Japanese city opened to European traders.

ISLAND ASIA

There are thousands of islands off the east coast of Asia. Many of them are grouped in arc-shaped, or curved, chains which curve outward from the Asian continent. There are three main island groups, each with several large islands and many smaller ones. They form the countries of Japan, the Philippines, and Indonesia.

Some of the other Asian islands are shown on the physical maps of Asia at the beginning of this volume. But others are too small to be shown on the map at all. On the map, many of the islands look close together. Actually, they may be hundreds of miles apart.

These islands which rim the eastern edge of Asia are the tops of great volcanic mountain ranges which were formed countless thousands of years ago. At certain places in the earth's crust there are weaknesses

called faults or fractures. Molten lava inside the earth forces its way through these weak places. The movement of the earth's crust and the eruption of molten lava cause tremendous shifts in the earth's surface.

Weak places in the earth's crust still exist in island Asia. From time to time earthquakes and volcanic eruptions occur on the islands, or on the floor of the ocean.

The seaward or Pacific side of these island mountain ranges is a series of ocean deeps or trenches. Some of the deepest places in the oceans of the world are here. In many places the ocean near these islands is more than 30,000 feet deep.

The three important island groups in east Asia—the Japanese islands, the Philippines, and the islands of the Republic of Indonesia—stretch from 45 degrees north to 10 degrees south of the equator. This is a distance of more than 4,000 miles. In spite of this great north-south distance, the three island groups have much in common.

These islands have fewer extremes of temperature than do large land areas on the continents. They have plenty of rainfall, although because of differences in latitude, the rains may fall at different times of the year. All three island groups are affected by severe storms called typhoons. Sometimes tidal waves accompany the typhoons, causing loss of life and property.

Because the islands are mountainous, they all have limited space for farming. Dense population is another characteristic of these island groups.

Every slope which can be terraced is made to grow food. Though the people and the crops differ from place to place, similar primitive farming methods are still used. Most of the work is done by hand rather than by machines. The slopes of most of the mountains in the islands are heavily forested. Valuable stands of timber are an important resource.

Because of their nearness to large continental countries, as well as their closeness to each other, the islands are in favorable locations as trade centers.

The greatest difference between these islands is among the people. Though most of the people are Asian in origin, they differ in many ways—different religions and degrees of civilization, different types of culture, and different races and colors.

Some primitive tribes still live in the interior jungles of the Celebes, Borneo, and the Philippines. But there are also people whose high degree of civilization and culture goes back in time for thousands of years. Furthermore, there has been a great mixture of cultures brought about by trade and by the movement of people from mainland countries to the islands.

Foreign countries owned many colonies among these islands and left their imprint on them. As a result, on these island groups live Japanese, Chinese, Hindus, Malayans, Arabians, Spanish, Portuguese, Dutch, British, and Americans.

Terraced rice-paddies allow Balinese farmers to use even sloping land for food production.

Wolfe Worldwide Films, Los Angeles 24, Calif.

Ernst A. Heiniger

Japanese farm workers, one wearing a thatched grass raincoat, cultivate hillside rice paddies.

Tidy rice fields and trees are typical in mountainous central Honshu, Japan's largest island.

Joe Barnell—Shostal

Using the Land and Sea

Japan's population of over 90 million people is crowded into less land than the New England states plus New York and New Jersey. Since three fourths of the land is mountainous, the problem of raising enough food is a constant one. Rice is cultivated intensively. More than half the cropland in Japan is used for growing rice. Japanese farmers, through hard work and careful cultivation, are able to grow more rice per acre than any other place in Asia.

In the warmer parts of Honshu and on the islands of Shikoku and Kyushu two crops of rice can be grown each year. Elsewhere in Japan one crop is raised during the warm, wet summer, and vegetables, sweet potatoes, and grains are grown on the dry fields after the rice is harvested.

Despite intensive cultivation, Japan must import large quantities of rice to feed her people. The Japanese raise few farm animals for food. Instead, they eat quantities of fish, and they can additional quantities of crabmeat, salmon, and other fish for export to other countries.

More than 19 million people live on the fertile, tropical, rainy Philippine Islands. Most of them are of Malayan stock. But unlike the Malays of Indonesia, most of the Filipinos are Christian, having been converted by Spanish Catholic missionaries long ago.

Many different languages are spoken by the tribes on remote islands and in distant mountain regions. The Igorots, who live in the highlands of Luzon, were headhunters until a few years ago. Pygmy Negritos live in the deep forests. Best known among the Filipino people are the Tagalogs, who make up the greater part of the population. Tagalog is the national language of the islands, though Spanish and English are spoken by many people in the cities.

Farming furnishes three fourths of the national income. The Filipino farmer is usually a tenant who works for a large land-

Ernst A. Heiniger

Girls carry seaweed to be dried and processed. Seaweed is important in the Japanese diet.

Ernst A. Heiniger

Japan's fishermen supply a major portion of the nation's food, as well as a leading export item.

owner. He lives in a farm village which is called a *barrio* and cultivates his rented land outside the *barrio*.

Sugar cane is the chief export crop, while rice and corn are the staple food crops. Coconut groves flourish on the sandy coastal plains.

The Philippines export great quantities of copra (dried coconut meat) and coconut oil used in the manufacture of soaps. The abacá plant furnishes fiber for Manila hemp, another valuable export. Forests which cover half the islands furnish valuable Philippine mahogany.

Long before Columbus discovered America, the Spice Islands were of great importance to the people of Europe. These tropical islands supplied Europe with pepper, cloves, nutmeg, cinnamon, and mace. Spices were almost worth their weight in gold, since they were the chief means of preserving meats. Nowadays, the Spice Islands (or the Moluccas as they are called today) still supply the world with spices. But they also supply the world with a great many other valuable agricultural products.

The Republic of Indonesia, a former Dutch possession, contains about 3,000 islands. Java, Sumatra, Celebes, and part of

Borneo are the largest land areas in Indonesia.

These tropical islands supply about one third of the world's natural rubber, three fourths of its kapok, almost all of its pepper and natural quinine, and large quantities of

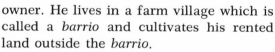

Kimonoed girls pick tea from well-trimmed bushes in Shizuoka Prefecture, central Honshu.

David Forbert—Shostal

Bundles of Manila hemp await shipment to factory. Hemp is a main export of the Philippines.

Philippine mahogany is a beautifully grained wood which is in demand for fine furniture.

Primitive Igorot tribesmen of northern Luzon still grind their grain in crude log mortars.

tea, coffee, and sugar. As in most warm, wet lands, rice is the important food crop for most of the people.

The chief agricultural island of Indonesia is Java. Java's main crop is rice. Rice paddies cover the fertile lowlands, and the hills are terraced for rice cultivation wherever enough water is available.

Much of the land in Java belongs to small farmers. The big estates, where most of the commercial export crops are grown, are mostly located in the uplands. Some export crops, such as tobacco and sugar, are also raised by small farmers.

The other islands are less densely populated than Java, and more of the cultivated land there is in large plantations.

Rubber and quinine once came only from the tropical rainforests of northern South America, where they were gathered from wild plants. But seeds were smuggled to Indonesia, and the Indonesian products soon crowded the South American ones off the world market. One reason was that it was cheaper to produce rubber and quinine on plantations than to gather them from the jungles. Another was that the quality of the plantation products, grown by skilled farmers, was better.

Primitive tribes live on many of these islands. Borneo, the third largest island in the world (only Greenland and New Guinea are larger), has comparatively few people. The Dyaks, many of whom were formerly headhunters, live in Borneo's dense forests, where they clear small patches of ground for homes and crude gardens. Dyaks live in "long houses" built high above the wet ground. Many families live in one house. Family "apartments" are separated by screens of banana leaves.

The Dyaks practice a primitive shifting agriculture, moving from place to place as the soil loses its fertility. They hunt wild animals, collect food from wild plants, tap wild rubber trees for latex, and plant a few foods by simply poking holes in the ground for seeds.

Gilloon Photo Agency

Dyak women perform household chores near a "long house" in Indonesia.

Gilloon Photo Agency

These cowboys of Jesselton, British North Borneo, are colorful individuals.

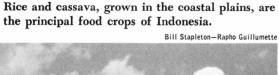

Rice and cassava, grown in the coastal plains, are the principal food crops of Indonesia.

Bill Stapleton—Rapho Guillumette

A fishing boat from a coastal village drops anchor off a tiny island in the Java Sea.

Van Bucher—Photo Researchers

Ewing Krainin—Photo Researchers

The silk industry is an old one in Japan. Here newly woven cloth is washed in a stream.

David Forbert—Shostal

The Miyata Seisakusho bicycle factory in Tokyo is an example of Japan's newer industries.

Industries of Island Asia

The rapid growth of industry in Japan is one of the wonders of the world. For hundreds of years Japan kept to herself, shut away from other countries. Yet today she is one of the ten leading industrial nations of the world and the leading industrial country in Asia. About one third of her income is from manufacturing. Over one fifth of the working population is engaged in some form of manufacturing.

Most of Japan's industry is centered in such big cities as Tokyo, Yokohama, Kyoto, Osaka, Kobe, and Nagasaki. A large part of Japan's manufacturing is done in small factories which employ fewer than five workers each. A great deal of the work is also done at home, in and around the large cities. This is Japan's "cottage industry." Part-time workers, especially women and girls, add to the family income by doing piecework in their homes.

Japan has few of the natural resources needed for large-scale manufacturing. Raw materials from the non-industrial nations of Asia are shipped to Japan and sold as manufactured goods to Asiatic countries and to the rest of the world. Workers are plentiful and labor is cheap. Thus Japan can afford to import raw materials and to sell manufactured goods at low prices.

Japan imports iron ore and rubber from southeast Asia; coke and coal from China; petroleum from Borneo and the Persian Gulf; and rice, sugar, and wheat from Formosa, Thailand, and Australia.

Japan manufactures a variety of light industrial products including textiles, chemicals, toys, sewing machines, bicycles, and tableware. Her workers are very skillful. Some of the finest radios, cameras, and optical goods are now exported to the United States.

Heavy steel industry is centered in northern Kyushu, which has the largest iron and

David Forbert—Shostal

Shipbuilding is an important industry to this island nation. This yard is at Nagasaki.

David Forbert—Shostal

Steel mills, like this one at Yawata, have become common sights in present-day Japan.

steel works in Japan. Japan's shipbuilding industry produces excellent ships.

Until recent years, less than one tenth of the Filipino workers were engaged in manufacture. Most of these performed some kind of handicraft. Industrial growth has been rapid since 1947.

Sugar, which was always the chief "money crop," was exported to the United States tax free. Today the islands must pay a tariff. As a result, they have had to turn to other industries and other markets to support their country.

Most of the manufacturing today is connected with processing agricultural products—sugar, coconut oil, rope, cigars, and canned pineapple. Other industries and better transportation, are being developed.

For the future the Philippines must improve farming methods so that more crops can be grown per acre. More food will have to be grown. Then the islands will not need to import so much.

Indonesia is a storehouse of natural wealth which has not been developed. These islands were for many years under foreign rule. Even today the Dutch, as well as Americans, British, and Chinese, have money invested in mines and plantations. The major part of their profits does not remain in the islands.

Tin, bauxite, and petroleum are three important mineral resources. But the islands hold vast untapped mineral reserves which only await development. Large estates still produce rubber, coffee, tea, kapok, cinchona, tobacco, and palm oil. Most of these products are processed in plantation factories and exported.

Though the Indonesian government is making great strides toward obtaining more benefits from foreign investments, the native population is still not able to operate these industries. For years to come, the industrial development of Indonesia will be in the hands of foreigners.

ASIA'S FUTURE

Great changes are taking place in Asia—perhaps more changes than on any other continent in the world. There are changes in the way some countries are governed. There are changes in the way many people live, and in the way they work and the kind of work they do. There are changes in education and health. And there are changes in the way people till the soil and in the appearance and the use of the land.

Some of these changes have happened quickly and recently. Others are just beginning to take shape and will not be complete for years to come. Many of the changes make life easier and better for the people. Some changes may not be good—

John Strohm

The face of this Chinese engineer reflects his country's determination to advance industrially.

Indonesians celebrate their independence with colorful parades and other demonstrations.

Van Bucher—Photo Researchers

only time will tell. Some things in Asia have not changed at all but should be changed if people are to live happy, healthy, and useful lives. And some things in Asia will probably never change.

Let us look at some of Asia's problems and some of the changes which are taking place. In this way we can look ahead to the future and imagine how Asia will solve her problems.

Some Asian countries were once colonies of European countries—England, France, and the Netherlands, for example. Even when the mother country governed well, most of the government jobs were in the hands of Europeans.

Few natives were trained for government work or for managing industry. In almost all the colonies there was a strong growth of nationalism—that is, the desire of the people to govern themselves. As these colonies won their independence, they faced new problems.

People had to be trained to fill government jobs, to run industries, to teach in schools, and to serve in hospitals. Some countries have kept European advisers to help them. Others are trying to run their governments and business affairs alone. Many Asian countries are receiving advice and help from the United Nations. Some countries are receiving help from the United States or from Soviet Russia.

For centuries some countries of Asia were ruled by kings or princes who had absolute power over the people. Most rulers of this type have been overthrown. But people in those countries have had little experience in democracy. They are still used to the strong-man type of government. There is danger in such places that dictators will take control.

In years to come there is no doubt that more and more Asians will be able to share in the responsibilities of their own government. The western democracies are ready to help the Asian people learn to use their new responsibilities for their own benefit.

Aramco—Photo Researchers

Geologists explore for oil in Saudi Arabia. Echoes from explosions help them to locate deposits.

Asia's transition from old to new is seen in these Buddhist monks waiting to board a plane.

Van Bucher—Photo Researchers

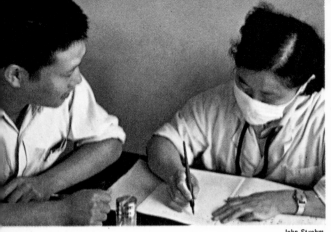

A technician records data on the health of a worker in a Peking textile mill.

Iranian children start their study of foreign languages at a very early age.

This Indian woman is a toxicologist, one who studies poisons and their antidotes.

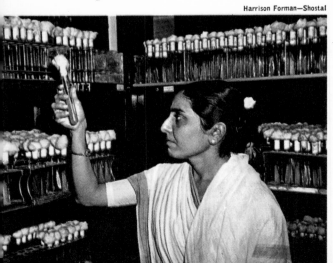

Education is an important problem in Asia. For hundreds of years, education was limited to the children of the small, ruling, wealthy class. Millions of Asians could not (and still cannot) read or write. There are still few public schools in most parts of Asia. However, great changes are beginning to take place.

Experts have been invited to some countries to plan new schools and better education. Older people are being taught to read and write. College students are being sent to universities in the United States, the Soviet Union, and Europe to complete their education. They are studying to be doctors, nurses, and teachers. When they return to their native lands they will teach others what they have learned. In time Asia will have its own schools and universities.

Some countries are adopting a simplified form of written language. Others are using a single common language to replace the hundreds of native dialects. The governments of Asian countries know that education for more people is vital if their countries are to take their place as equals among the nations of the world.

One of Asia's gravest problems is the sheer number of people who live there. There are so many people in Asia that there is never enough of the basic necessities of life—food, clothing, and housing—to go round.

In some regions many people live on the edge of starvation, dress in rags, and sleep in doorways and streets. Poverty prevents people from getting an education and improving their living standards. And the population of Asia grows so fast that improvements in food production never quite catch up with the number of mouths that have to be fed.

Health is another serious problem in Asia. In previous years disease and malnutrition have killed millions of people each year. The death rate in Asia has always been high, and, though the birth rate is very high, millions of babies die each year.

Tony Chapelle—Monkmeyer

Under Point IV, medical assistance is supplied to the Middle East by American doctors.

Kulwant Roy

New power plants like this one in India will supply power for factories and homes.

Tropical diseases of many kinds are common. Blindness afflicts millions. Plagues wipe out entire villages. Furthermore, ignorance and habit have made many people in Asia afraid of new ideas and new ways to treat disease. Their religions have often made them accept disease and death as something to be expected and accepted.

Today there are new medical discoveries which are saving millions of lives. United Nations agencies have sent doctors, nurses, and scientists as well as medical supplies to many parts of Asia. Inoculations, antibiotics, and vitamins are saving millions of lives each year.

But solving the problem of health conditions creates a new problem. The lives saved by medical advances add to the problem of population pressure. In the future Asia will need to cope with the problem of training her own doctors and nurses to continue the work of health improvement. And she will need to solve the problem of feeding and housing the millions of additional people who are being saved by medical science.

Most people in Asia have always made their living from the land. They are farmers or herders of flocks. Before World War II only Japan had a high degree of industrialization. In other Asian countries, industries were based on hand labor. Factories were given over mainly to processing food and other agricultural products. Large-scale production was centered on colonial estates. Industrial plants were managed by European people. Few Asians were employed in industry, except in the most menial tasks.

In the future Asia will be busy training her people to manage industries, to develop better mechanical skills, to rely on industry as well as on agriculture for their living. Foreign capital is still invested in Asian industry. But more and more Asians are learning crafts and trades which will make it easier for them to make a better living in the future.

Great changes are taking place in agriculture. Farmers in many countries now own their own land. New methods, new tools, better fertilizer, and improved seeds

Communist China celebrates the opening of a new stadium in Peking with elaborate ceremonies.

will produce more crops. Great irrigation projects and dams for water and water power are being built in many parts of Asia. Land which is now almost desert will be made to grow food.

Asia will probably remain largely an agricultural region, but the future will bring great improvements in the amount of food raised, the kinds of crops raised, and the returns which the average Asian farmer will receive from his labor.

Vast stores of minerals lie buried in central Asia. Many of these minerals are located in places that can hardly be reached today. Metallic ores are often found far from deposits of the fuel needed to refine them. Transportation is not available to

move the ores to industrial centers. And much of central Asia is not yet mapped.

But China and the Soviet Union are making geological surveys to locate new mineral deposits. And improved rail, highway, and air transportation will make it possible to tap the mineral resources which now lie hidden in central Asia.

American and European geologists are finding new, untapped petroleum deposits in Arabia, Iraq, and Iran. As these oil discoveries are developed, some of the profits from them will probably be used for the benefit of the people of the Middle East.

Communism is a problem which affects the entire world. Asia has been the scene of great Communist influence. Part of this is

An interior view of a general store, typical of those found on Chinese Communist communes

Planting in a garden near Peking, children learn to work with hands as well as heads.

the result of Soviet Russia's efforts to woo the people by sending them advisers who speak the native language, and by lending money, machines, and experts.

But the free world is doing much to stop the spread of Communism in Asia. Western democracies have spent billions of dollars to help develop Asia's resources. Dams and power projects, mineralogical surveys, studies to improve crops, and programs to improve health and education have been supported by many nations.

The free people of the world are trying through programs of help and advice to sway Asian countries toward western democracy and western ideas.

Today it is no longer possible for one part of the world to avoid being affected by what happens in other parts.

Asia is a continent rich in natural resources which the world needs. The oil, rubber, drugs, foods, tin, and other minerals are eagerly sought by European and American countries.

Manufactured goods must be sold. The future will continue to see competition among the nations of the world for Asia's raw materials and for her markets.

The people of Asia are eager for equality and respect. They have always objected to the way many western countries looked down upon them. The brown, yellow, and black-skinned people of Asia will continue to seek equality and respect from the United States and other nations over the world. The future of Western relations with Asia depends on how well we can change our own attitudes and accept Asian countries as equals.

As education increases, and as opportunities occur for making a better living, the lives of millions of Asians will improve. People in other parts of the world are conscious of Asia's importance to them. They are helping Asia for Asia's good. At the same time the United States and other nations realize that what helps Asia also helps the rest of the world.

Children at a co-operative school in Taiwan (Formosa) follow their teacher in a medley of songs.

Hamilton Wright Organization, Inc.

ASIA—FACTS AND FIGURES

PRINCIPAL COUNTRIES: AREA AND POPULATION

Country	Area in sq. miles	Population (est. 1960)
Afghanistan	250,000	13,000,000
Burma	261,750	20,685,600
Cambodia	69,000	5,000,000
Ceylon	25,332	9,737,500
China (Communist)	3,760,000	679,630,000
Formosa (Nationalist China)	13,885	10,483,800
India	1,266,000	407,732,500
Indonesia	575,890	89,584,000
Iran	630,000	20,050,000
Iraq	168,000	6,656,100
Israel	8,000	2,070,000
Japan	141,000	93,196,000
Jordan	37,000	1,643,200
Korea, North	47,000	10,353,000
Korea, South	37,000	22,909,200
Laos	91,450	1,707,960
Lebanon	4,000	1,596,500
Malaya	50,600	6,701,500
Nepal	54,000	9,100,000
Pakistan	364,700	87,797,500
Philippines	115,700	23,946,500
Saudi Arabia	600,000	7,121,300
Syria (United Arab Republic)	72,200	4,359,600
Thailand	198,500	24,591,400
Turkey	299,000	27,268,500
Vietnam, North	60,900	14,630,500
Vietnam, South	66,350	12,410,700

LARGE CITIES AND THEIR POPULATION

City and Country	Est. Pop.
Tokyo, Japan	8,774,700
Shanghai, China	6,204,400
Peking, China	4,140,000
Tientsin, China	3,100,000
Calcutta, India	2,982,000
Bombay, India	2,840,000
Jakarta, Indonesia	2,800,000
Osaka, Japan	2,632,000
Hong Kong, China	2,600,000
Shenyang (Mukden), China	2,290,000
New Delhi, India	2,000,000
Teheran, Iran	1,957,600
Wuhan, China	1,800,000
Canton, China	1,650,000
Chungking, China	1,620,000
Seoul, South Korea	1,574,900
Madras, India	1,416,100
Nagoya, Japan	1,387,000
Baghdad, Iraq	1,306,600
Singapore, Malaya	1,236,000
Kyoto, Japan	1,210,100
Manila, Philippines	1,200,000
Yokohama, Japan	1,182,200
Karachi, Pakistan	1,126,400
Nanking, China	1,114,000
Hyderabad, India	1,085,700
Dairen, China	1,054,000
Pusan, South Korea	1,049,370

HIGHEST MOUNTAINS AND THEIR ELEVATIONS

Mountain and Country	Height in feet
Everest, Nepal-Tibet	29,028
K2 (Godwin Austen), India	28,250
Kanchenjunga, Nepal-Sikkim	28,150
Makalu, Nepal-Tibet	27,800
Cho Oyu, Nepal-Tibet	26,867

LARGEST LAKES AND THEIR AREAS

Lake and Country	Area in sq. miles
Urmia, Iran	2,300
Koko Nor, China	2,200
Hamun-i-Helmand, Afghanistan-Iran	2,000
Van, Turkey	2,000
Tungting, China	1,450

LONGEST RIVERS AND THEIR LENGTH

River and Region of Asia	Length in miles
Yangtze, Interior-Eastern	3,100
Hwang Ho, Interior-Eastern	2,800
Mekong, Southeastern	2,700
Indus, Southern	1,900
Brahmaputra, Interior-Southern	1,800
Salween, Southern	1,750
Euphrates, Southwestern	1,700
Ganges, Southern	1,560
Irrawaddy, Southern	1,400